To: My friend ~Barb~
Who was there when
I needed her.

Love
Anneke
2016

PRAISE FOR *LIVING THE BRAVEHEART LIFE*

"There are two ways a writer can be brave. One, he can tackle a daunting and ambitious subject. Two, he can write in his own voice, revealing for the benefit of his readers private and dangerous stuff about his own psyche, his life, his struggles. Then there's a third way (and I didn't know this till I read *Living the Braveheart Life*). That way is acting with courage in his real life.

"Randall Wallace has done all three in this extraordinary new book. I don't think I've ever read anything like it. *Living the Braveheart Life* is a prescription for what ails the contemporary soul, and no one but Mr. Wallace could have written it. It's his testament as a father and a son, as a Scot and a Southerner, and as a writer . . . straight from a brave, brave heart."

—STEVEN PRESSFIELD, SCREENWRITER AND BESTSELLING
AUTHOR, *GATES OF FIRE* AND *THE WAR OF ART*

"Randall Wallace is a man who approaches filmmaking with great care and passion. We've enjoyed working on a number of films together over the years, and I can tell you one thing for certain: he has a natural intuition as to what makes a truly great story. *Living the Braveheart Life* will show you how a true master craftsman approaches storytelling and life with great courage."

—DEAN SEMLER, AM. ACS. ASC., ACADEMY AWARD–WINNING
CINEMATOGRAPHER, *SECRETARIAT*, *DANCES WITH WOLVES*, *THE PATRIOT*

"The creator of the epics *Braveheart* and *We Were Soldiers* takes us on a personal journey that is no less inspiring than those of his movie characters. Informative, entertaining, and ultimately spiritual, Randall Wallace reminds us what truly matters."

—STANLEY MCCHRYSTAL, GEN., US ARMY (RET.),
BESTSELLING AUTHOR, *TEAM OF TEAMS*

"The essence of the Braveheart Life is courage, sacrifice, selflessness, and choosing to live not for yourself but for other people, in freedom, the way God intended. *Living the Braveheart Life* is the only way to truly live."

—SEAN HANNITY, #1 *NEW YORK TIMES* BESTSELLING
AUTHOR AND HOST, *HANNITY*, FOX NEWS

"If C. S. Lewis had been blessed with a Tennessee birth, a Virginia upbringing, and a career in Hollywood, he might have written this book. If you loved *Braveheart* as much as I did, then you will be enthralled with the journey that pushed Randall Wallace to write it."

—JILL CONNER BROWNE, #1 *NEW YORK TIMES* BESTSELLING
AUTHOR, SWEET POTATO QUEENS SERIES

"Randy Wallace is an American treasure. He lives the Braveheart Life, so I'm glad that by reading this book, others will have the chance to try to live it too."

—LAURA INGRAHAM, HOST, *THE LAURA INGRAHAM SHOW*

"*Braveheart* isn't just a film by Randall Wallace—it's a portrayal of a life well-lived because of the heart found in its hero. By all accounts Randall is an iconic writer and filmmaker who has achieved stratospheric success. At the same time he is one of the most down-to-earth people you will ever meet. No one can better communicate the ups and downs, the joys and struggles, or the costs and rewards of building your own Braveheart Life. Read this book. You'll be glad you did."

—TODD BURPO, PASTOR, VOLUNTEER FIREMAN, AND
#1 *NEW YORK TIMES* BESTSELLING AUTHOR, *HEAVEN IS FOR REAL*

LIVING THE
BRAVEHEART
LIFE

LIVING THE BRAVEHEART LIFE

Finding the Courage to Follow Your Heart

RANDALL WALLACE

W Publishing Group

AN IMPRINT OF THOMAS NELSON

Published in Nashville, Tennessee, by W Publishing Group, an imprint of Thomas Nelson.

Thomas Nelson titles may be purchased in bulk for educational, business, fund-raising, or sales promotional use. For information, please e-mail SpecialMarkets@ ThomasNelson.com.

Unless otherwise noted, Scripture quotations are taken from the New King James Version. © 1982 by Thomas Nelson, Inc. Used by permission. All rights reserved.

Scripture quotations marked KJV are from the King James Version of the Bible.

Library of Congress Cataloging-in-Publication Data

Wallace, Randall.
    Living the Braveheart life: finding the courage to follow your heart / Randall Wallace.
        pages cm
    ISBN 978-0-7180-3147-3 (hardback)
1. Authors, American—20th century—Biography. I. Wallace, Randall. II. Title.
    PS3573.A429Z46 2015
    813'.54—dc23
    [B]
                                                2015007225

Printed in the United States of America

15 16 17 18 19 RRD 6 5 4 3 2 1

Before the release of *Heaven Is for Real*, friends in Mississippi helped arrange an advanced screening, and among those in attendance were some young people whose only home is the palliative care unit of the Blair Batson Memorial Children's Hospital. They are paralyzed from the neck down, their bodies confined to wheelchairs.

At the end of the screening one of the nurses, who has become family to these children, asked one of them, a luminous girl named D'Asia, what she thought of the movie. D'Asia replied, "I felt God was right in my face."

This book is dedicated to everyone who has placed God right in my face. To the Teachers and Friends who have shared their lessons and their hearts, and the enemies who have taught me too. To the heroes of the past and the poets who have shaped their Stories into a history that can speak to me. To those like my Grandmother, and my Father and Mother, whose love bore the nature of Divinity in its constant and eternal Presence, even when I could not see their eyes and touch their faces. And to my sons—Andrew, Cullen, and Soren Eli—whose very presence sings anthems of the love of God.

CONTENTS

Preface: Gathering Around the Fire. xi

Introduction: The Freedom to Scream "Freeeeeedommmm!" xv

PART I: FATHERS AND SONS

   1 A Father's Stories 3

   2 The Father 11

   3 The Men—and the Women—Who Made My Father a Man. . . 17

   4 A Calling 21

   5 A Calling—and a Piano-Playing Pig 27

   6 Bob from Afghanistan 33

   7 Brothers and Sisters. 43

   8 Art and the Braveheart Life 47

   9 Where the Finger Points 55

PART II: THE ROAD TO *Braveheart*

   10 Alpha and Omega 69

   11 The Mother. 77

   12 Connecting: The Power of True Partnership 81

CONTENTS

PART III: THE WAYS OF THE WARRIOR

13 Never Stop Learning. And Never Stop Teaching. 87

14 Lessons Are Sometimes Harsh. 95

15 A Warrior Is Always Asking, "What Is a Warrior?" 103

16 The Warrior and Love. 109

17 The Braveheart Life Embraces Mystery 115

18 A Warrior Believes. 121

19 My Daddy's Gift 129

PART IV: THE HOLES IN OUR ARMOR

20 In Defense of Fear 137

21 The Fears of Women 145

22 Fear's Greatest Lie 149

23 Losing Our Identity 153

PART V: OUTLAW CHRISTIANITY

24 Huck Finn: The Great Outlaw 163

25 Jumping Jack Flash 169

26 Milano 171

27 *Living* the Braveheart Life. 179

28 Where Do You Put Your Guns? 187

29 So Who Goes to Heaven? 193

PART VI: VICTORY

30 Love Transforms. 199

31 Ego. 203

Notes. 213

About the Author. 217

GATHERING AROUND THE FIRE

ON AN EARLY SUMMER DAY IN IRELAND TWO DECADES AGO, I stood on a field, where a film crew was re-creating a massive fight that had taken place seven hundred years earlier. The fight was the Battle of Stirling, and the movie was *Braveheart*.

It was the first time I had ever seen something I had written becoming a feature film.

For that moment we had gathered together more than two thousand Irish Extras to play the Scottish Highlanders who had fought that day. They were members of the IRA—not the one you think about when you hear those letters—the Irish Reserve Army. As reservists, they were required to put in a few weeks of military drill each year. The production team had made a deal with the Irish government to let us use these hordes of young men: they got to work on a movie instead of doing monotonous military drills, and the film company benefitted by having inexpensive labor for the big battle scenes of the movie.

My father-in-law's ancestors were all Irish, and in my experience the people who come from that magical island are a kind of rolling chaos; wherever two or more are gathered, it is a fight or a party—or both. It didn't take much to change the modern Irishmen into Highland warriors; they came ready-made with the right haircuts and the right tattoos. The film's makeup artists didn't even have to smear dirt on most of them. The Assistant Directors had lined them up in rough formation, and the Extras were doing what Irishmen love to do; they were playing, whacking one another with the rubber swords and rubber spears we'd given them.

In all fairness they had every right to be bored. Veterans of the movie business say the most exciting day of your life is your first day on a movie set; the most boring day of your life is your second. This was their third day of standing in lines, posing in the background to establish the masses of men who had fought the great battle we were all there to capture.

That same morning they had stood for hours in the background as the crew filmed close-ups of the conferences of the Scottish noblemen who were ready to sell out the commoners in order to gain concessions from the English king. The one bit of action the Irish Extras had gotten to portray was the beginning of the mutiny of the Scottish army; they were allowed to shift positions, beginning to walk away, just before William Wallace would arrive with his band of Highland rebels.

The Extras then had to stand in place again, doing nothing, as the crew placed seven cameras in position to film that arrival. That took time too; the process of filming can be profoundly tedious for those not directly involved in setting angles and focus and light reflectors. By now the Irishmen were ready to go to the pubs and party in earnest.

And then something happened. One of the Assistant Directors shouted, "Action!" and Mel Gibson came riding out on a horse. He was dressed as William Wallace, his face half covered in blue woad, the battle paint of Scottish warriors.

I, along with all the film crew and Irish Extras on the field that day, gasped. He was no longer an actor; he was not a man playing another man; he was the man he was portraying; he *was* William Wallace. The wind was whipping his hair across his face, and the horse could feel his adrenaline and was darting left and right. Almost as one, those two thousand Irishmen sucked in air and fell silent. I did too—it was the kind of moment that made you want to hold your breath.

The warrior on the horse stopped in front of the men facing him. His eyes, burning with passion, swept the horde before him, and he shouted, "Sons of Scotland! I am William Wallace! And I see before me a whole army of my countrymen, come in defiance of tyranny! You've come to fight as free men—and free men you are! But what will you do with your Freedom? Will you fight?!" These were words I had written a year before, in America.

The Irish Extras had been well instructed by a corps of Assistant Directors and production assistants; they had been clearly told that at that moment they were to stand frozen as another actor—strategically placed among them, in the right position for the seven cameras that were running—stepped forward and cried out that the English were too many and that they would run, and live. This would allow for the rest of the speech I had written for William Wallace:

> "Aye. Fight, and you may die. Run, and you'll live—at least awhile. And dying in your beds many years from now, would you not trade all the days from that day to this, for one chance—just one chance!—to come back here and tell our enemies that they may take our lives . . . but they'll never take our Freedom!"

That was what was *supposed* to happen. What did happen was those Irish actors stood there in that moment, drinking in those words. And when they heard, "You've come to fight as free men, and free men you are! But what will you do with your Freedom? Will you fight?!" all two thousand of those Irishmen screamed out, "Yes! We'll kill 'em all!!!"

Then the man on the horse transformed from William Wallace back to Mel Gibson, and the Assistant Directors, production assistants, and camera crews yelled, "Cut! Cut! Cut!" Seven times, "*Cut!*" and they all began to explain to the Extras, "Now, fellas, this is just a movie. You don't get to kill anybody today."

With great reluctance, and a disappointment verging on despair, the Irishmen formed up again and stood there dutifully until, at the appropriate place at last, they could scream their hearts out.

That is the way I remember the event. Others who were there that day surely remember it somewhat differently. But I felt that moment in the same way the Irishmen did. In fact, I felt the moment before the Irishmen did. I felt it when I wrote it.

How I came to write that moment is part of this story. Another part is what I learned from living through the events, and maybe an even bigger part—certainly a more important part to you—is what you might learn from these moments, and the events surrounding them, bringing them into being and propelling the consequences of the passions surrounding them.

I related to the Irishmen that day. I felt as one with them and certainly felt as one with William Wallace. Many men, and women, too, have found a central part of themselves expressed in that story and especially in that moment.

Something was at work then, Something that had the Power to transform boredom into passion, Death into Life.

Don't we all look for such a place like the one I believe William Wallace and the men who fought beside him were in that day? Isn't there something in you and me that craves, needs, *demands* us to seek to stand for something more important than our own little lives—to stand for the Great Life in the hand of God?

This is a book about that *Something*. This is a book about the Braveheart Life.

INTRODUCTION

THE FREEDOM TO SCREAM "FREEEEEEDOMMMM!"

I RECENTLY BUILT A NEW HOME. I LOVE FIRES AND FIREPLACES and the talks and silences that happen around them. Etched into the stone above the mantel of my new fireplace is a single word: *FREEDOM!*

Of all the words that mark *Braveheart* in the spirits of those who have been moved by the story, that single word represents its essence more than any other.

When I first went to Scotland in search of my roots, I found that another Wallace—William Wallace—had walked the Highlands seven hundred years before. I also discovered that my family had a coat of arms—a big surprise, when your family comes from Lizard Lick, Tennessee. And we had a family motto: *Pro Libertate*—For Freedom. And that was no surprise at all.

Freedom has always been the Holy Grail at the center of my life. One of Jesus' most captivating statements for me was always: "Ye shall know the truth, and the truth shall make you free."[1]

So in this story I would like to tell you the truth. I would like to tell you as faithfully and freely as I can how *Braveheart* came to life—where it came from and where it seems to be leading me now.

To do this, I will speak about Fathers and Mothers too. About Teachers, Warriors, and Sacred Men—and Women. You don't need to be male to have a seat at the fireplace and open your heart. In fact, it is a great piece of the Truth to understand that men and women aren't complete without each other.

One of the most moving moments I ever experienced regarding *Braveheart* was at a charity screening in Austin, Texas, a few years ago. I had not shown the movie in a full theater in many years, and about half the audience there that evening had never seen the film.

At the end of the screening, I was to conduct a question-and-answer session, and during it a young woman—only nineteen, who had barely been born when the movie first came out—stood up from the front row and said, "Mr. Wallace, I don't have a question. I just want to tell you something. My fiancé died six months ago. And before he died, he told me he wanted me to see *Braveheart* so I would understand the way he loved me."

So the Stories I will tell you now around this fireplace of the heart won't be a careful, academic treatise. I would like to speak as honestly and openly as I would if you and I were sitting at my fireplace in front of that single word that means so much. Maybe together we can find not just truth but a great Truth.

And together we can find *FREEDOM!*

TALES AROUND THE FIRE

> *To Scottish friends I lift a glass*
> *To you, who've kept alive*
> *The memory of heroes past*
> *Across dark moors of time.*
>
> *To you who know this simple truth,*
> *And show it near and far:*
> *It is the tales we tell ourselves*
> *That make us who we are.*

So let us drink to Scotland fair
Its sorrows and its solace
And lift our glasses in the air
To you, and William Wallace

And all of you who feel the same
My sisters and my brothers
I'd rather be a man in your eyes
Than a king in any others.
—RANDALL WALLACE, *BRAVEHEART*,
THE NOVEL, DEDICATION

There are four father/son relationships in *Braveheart*. William Wallace and his Father are the first. We also find his best friend, Hamish, and his Father, both of whom fight alongside William Wallace. Then there is Robert the Bruce, whose father is dying of leprosy while trying to guide his son to the throne of Scotland. And the final father/son relationship is that of King Edward I of England, Longshanks, who is so deeply disappointed and hostile to Edward II.

Then, of course, there is also Stephen of Ireland, who constantly and openly talks to God, referring to him directly as "Father!"

Uncle Argyle is not William's father. But when the boy is left fatherless, Argyle steps into that role, and in doing so he manifests every aspect of the Braveheart Spirit.

The Father is love, attention, strength, loyalty. But he is so much more than any list of traits. A Father and a Mother are, at first, *everything*—that's how it feels to the parents, if not to the children. Anyone who is a father or a mother knows the feeling of massive responsibility that comes with the initial stages of parenthood, the overwhelming sense that all our children are or ever will become is in our hands. Later comes the humility—maybe even a sense of helplessness—that helps us realize the child has an identity, a purpose, a destiny that is separate from us.

To the boy, at first, the Father is a model. He stands in front of the boy as a demonstration of the manhood the boy is meant to achieve and maintain.

Young William Wallace wanted to be like his father. When he sees his father riding off with his brother to go perform a manly duty—checking on the neighbors he had not heard from since they went off to a meeting at the summons of the king—the boy wants to go with them. His father is proud of his son's spirit; he refuses his son's request but validates his manly desires, using them as an opportunity for a lesson: "I know! I know you can fight! But it's our wits that make us men."

Little does the father know how soon his son will need this lesson.

The boy goes anyway, disobeying his father's instructions but not his father's spirit. He sees the kind of sight that his father would have always wanted to spare him: a scene of just how ugly humans can be to one another, inside a barn where Scottish patriots—the Wallaces' independent-minded neighbors—have been hanged.

That night the boy overhears his father's leadership, urging his remaining neighbors to make a demonstration of their resolve. "We don't have to beat them," William's father tells his friends. "Only show them that we will fight."

The next day William's father is dead. When Uncle Argyle appears, William immediately recognizes him as his father's true brother, a man who shares his father's Braveheart Spirit.

Truth is one of the greatest of strengths, and it is with truth that Argyle begins. He reminds young William of all the realities facing them, however harsh.

In giving the boy the truth, the Father—for such has Argyle in this moment become—calls manhood from the boy: "Your father is dead. You didn't want it to happen, but here it is. We must move ahead."

But Argyle is not without his tenderness. He asks about the most reverent of expressions, the prayers at the graves. The prayers that he finds most sacred to his own family he prays at the boy's bedside. He reveals to the boy the greater depths of life.

And when the boy moves outside the house, stepping from the warmth of bed and hearth into the outer world of cold and shadow, he finds his uncle there, bonded in his spirit to the heart of the clansmen who participate in their shared sacred ritual. When the boy reaches for the blade, Argyle, now the boy's spiritual father, resonates with the wisdom of William's bodily father's admonition: "It's our wits that make us men."

This scene gives me goosebumps. To say that must seem the pinnacle of pride, since I am credited with its authorship.

But the scene was not written by me, it was written through me— or, more precisely, on me and in me by men in my life, especially by my own Father.

In this book I will speak of my Father's life, of my Mother's, of the lives of Friends who have shared their deepest heart with me. And yet I don't mean this story as biography or even as history, any more than I wanted *Braveheart* to qualify as such things.

I think it's fair to say that what I want this book to be about is not so much me, but about you, the reader. Anyone *Braveheart* connects with does not love the story for what it says about William Wallace, or about Randall Wallace, for that matter; they love the story because when they experience it, they feel the rising of their own Braveheart.

The Stories we think of as great stories are the ones we retell. They go forward into the future, shaping us and new generations. The Stories also come from places of heartbreak and hope, despair and faith, fear and love.

Here, around this spiritual campfire of ours, beneath the stone carved with the word *FREEDOM!* I want to share some of the Stories that shaped *Braveheart* and what they have taught me about the Braveheart Life.

There is power in Stories. And my stories may be interesting to you, in the same way that *Braveheart* might have interested you. But of far greater power to you are not my stories but yours. Which Stories have you heard that shape your life? What do you believe? I mean what you *really* believe, when you are asked to lift the Swords in your life, or lay them down. What makes you who you are?

We can find answers in the Stories we tell.

What I will tell you in the pages that follow, sitting at this spiritual fire of ours, are some of my Stories—the Stories that make me who I am. My hope is that they will cause you to reflect on your own Stories, the ones that make you who you are. In doing this, those old Stories can grow richer and deeper. And newer.

PART I

FATHERS AND SONS

ONE

A Father's Stories

On a late summer day in the early 1920s, not long after the First World War, a strong young Tennessean named Jesse Wallace was hunting through a woodland near his family's farm. The forests were thick with pecan trees and oaks. The leaves were lush in mid-July.

Jesse carried a shotgun. His new father-in-law, Jake Rhodes, could knock squirrels out of the treetops with a .22 caliber rifle, but few men, even Tennesseans, were that quick and accurate with a light rifle. Jesse preferred the decisiveness, the quick pull and bang of a 12-guage shotgun. He liked strolling the woods, and he enjoyed providing the meat for dinner.

He shot easily and calmly and deliberately, never wasting a shot. He had enough squirrels to fill his game bag when he turned for home. He was warm from the hunt and the walk, and he was thirsty too. So a couple of miles from the farmhouse he knelt down and lapped a cool drink from a spring.

The next day he came down with typhoid fever. He speculated with his family, before he became delirious, that the fever must've come from that stream; there were no other cases of it in the family or among immediate neighbors. His family was worried, of course, but none was as concerned as Jesse's new wife, Lena, who was just seventeen, a bride for barely a year.

The nearest town was called Henderson, and the doctor who came out to the Wallaces' farm treated typhoid in the accepted practice of the day, with purgatives. The doctor dosed him with something called ipecac, which caused him to vomit. He grew so weak the treatment was suspended. He began to grow stronger—strong enough to resume the treatment. He died, probably of dehydration from the vomiting.

Lena was two months pregnant at the time of Jesse's death. She may not have even been sure she was expecting when she became a widow.

The child in her belly was my father. She would name him Jesse Thurman. The Wallaces would call the boy Jesse, in memory of his father. But Lena, when she moved back to live with her Rhodes family, would call her son Thurman. To even speak the name Jesse broke her heart.

So my father grew up without a father. And how he became the greatest of fathers is one of life's great marvels for me. Daddy— Southerners of my vintage call their fathers "Daddy" throughout life—would drive me to the graveyard whenever we visited the area of his birth, and we would stand at the stone with the name Jesse Wallace cut deep into its surface. Daddy seldom spoke at those moments, one of the rare times when he was silent about anything. After five-minute eternities of such quiet, when the wind would whisper through the trees and grasshoppers grated in the grass at the cemetery's fringes, he would lead us back to the Oldsmobile, and we would drive back home. A mood, not sadness exactly but something like longing and loneliness, would cloak him like a morning fog. But the rumble of the Rocket V-8 and the Olds dancing down the swaying road would bring the sunshine back to his eyes, and he would tell me stories as he always did.

IN OUR FAMILY WE LOVED STORIES. EVERYONE ALWAYS SAID the Wallaces were good at telling them.

My Mother's family had a story too—a massive mystery, never mentioned, never hinted at—a secret hidden through generations, one that ricochets through my life even now.

But that is a story I am not yet ready to share—largely because it is a story I still don't know enough about and may never understand. My Mother's family knew how to maintain a great Silence on personal matters, meaning everything pertaining to family. She was as inward as my Father was outgoing. And in this she taught me a powerful truth: the most potent stories contain the mysterious, and Silence can be loud.

⊰⊱⊰⊱⊰⊱

YEARS AFTER JESSE WALLACE DIED, A YOUNG WRITER TRAVELING in Scotland would first encounter a legend about another man named Wallace—the same name the writer carried. The writer's name was Randall Wallace; grandson of Jesse, son of Thurman. Yours truly.

I was about to become a father for the first time. I had married a woman who knew the exact counties in Ireland where her father's forebears had been born. Her mother's people were Mormons, and they could trace their ancestors back for centuries.

All I knew of my Father's people was that they came from Lizard Lick, Tennessee. The men in my Father's family were Alton, Elton, Dalton, Lymon, Gleamon, Herman, Thurman (my Daddy), and Clyde. They called Clyde "Pete," and nobody knew why. (I am not making this up.) But they were all on the Rhodes side of the family. The history of the Wallaces that I knew of hit a wall at the death of Jesse, my Daddy's Daddy.

There were three great disconnects for me in knowing my ancestry—one general to all Southerners, and two highly specific to my family and profoundly mysterious to me. The general disconnect

5

is that the American South, both ethnically and culturally, is largely Scottish. The reason for this (being mostly unknown) is that the great Scottish migration to North America began long before there was a United States. Warrior clans of the Scottish Highlands, starved by the encroachment of the rising empire controlled by the English, saw opportunity in the new colonies of the New World, and they came as soldiers, sailors, and indentured servants. Pioneers and Indian fighters like Davy Crockett and Daniel Boone, as well as a great swath of presidents, including Andrew Jackson, Ronald Reagan, and Bill Clinton, have Scottish ancestry. But from the beginning the Scots coming to the New World did not hyphenate their heritage as others did; they were not Irish-Americans or Italian-Americans or Jewish- or African- or Japanese-Americans; they just called themselves Americans. I grew up completely unaware of my Scottish roots.

But the other two disconnects in my knowledge of heritage were far more specific. They were the death of my Grandfather before my Father was born and the mysterious Silence of my Mother concerning her own lineage.

I decided to search for my own roots so that I could share my side of the story with my new son who was on the way. The term *roots* had taken on greater meaning because of the spectacularly powerful and successful television miniseries first broadcast when I began dating the woman I would eventually marry. She was born and raised in Los Angeles, a brilliant woman who had quit a job as a social worker to launch a career dancing on television and in movies. Like most Californians, she saw the South as a kind of hillbilly cartoon, where we stopped watching Professional Rasslin' and TV evangelists only long enough to eat grits and spit through the gaps in our teeth. She also, however, seemed to think that some Southern boys were studs. I was crazy about her.

Roots was such a powerful experience that it captivated America, and in the days before people could record television shows and view them at any time, we would all gather to watch the new airing of each episode. I was in my future wife's apartment with her brother and sister when *Roots* reached a climax: the central character, Kunta Kinte, had tried to flee captivity, but slave chasers captured him, and in one horrific moment they took a hatchet to his foot and severed its front half so he could never run again.

We all sat watching this in silent horror, sitting around a television set in Sherman Oaks, sipping white wine—until the slave chaser lifted his hatchet and chopped into Kunta Kinte's foot.

In that moment I realized that all three of the Californians in the room had turned, silent and appalled, to stare—at me.

<hr/>

I WOULD LATER HEAR THAT MEMBERS OF MY FAMILY HAD fought on both sides of the Civil War. (But that's another story.) When I went to Scotland, my only clue of any ancestor beyond my Grandfathers, both of them dead before I was born, was from a cousin who had gone to Europe while in the army and had returned to report that he'd heard somebody named Wallace had come from Scotland.

So it was to Scotland that I headed, my pregnant wife in tow. (To be honest, I was the one in tow; she could plan anything and loved to travel and organize.) We went to Edinburgh, the most picturesque of British cities, and walked into the castle there, simply because I loved castles and history and windswept pinnacles like the one where the castle sat.

We'd just started through the main entrance, an archway into the courtyard of the castle, and I stopped short. Flanking the entrance were two bold statues. One was Robert the Bruce, Scotland's most famous king.

The other was clearly a warrior, clad in armor. The inscription at the base of the statue just said "Wallace."

I grabbed my wife's arm as I pointed to the statue and said to a passing guard, "This Wallace . . . who is he?"

The guard was a member of the Black Watch and wore a kilt made of the tartan unique to his regiment. He was short and stood with his feet spread wide, looking as if you could slam his head with a sledgehammer and drive him into the flagstones like a spike, whole and unscathed. In a Highland burr he answered, "That is William Wallace—our grrrreatest herrrrrrro!"

Greatest hero! Wallace! I glanced at my wife to see if she was as impressed as I was.

She wasn't.

"So this William Wallace . . ." I asked Mr. Black Watch. "His dates overlap Robert the Bruce." I knew from my lifelong fascination with history that the Bruce was Scotland's greatest king, renowned in poetry for his courage and persistence. "Were Wallace and Bruce allies in fighting the English?"

"No one will ever know for sure," he said, magic words for any writer, "but our legends say the Bruce may have been one of those who betrayed William Wallace, to clear the way for him to become king himself."

I can see that moment now, my wife and I standing in the gray castle beneath a gray Scottish sky, our first son growing in her belly. I can't say the colors grew brighter or that I saw them as suddenly deeper, but something changed. I had discovered something—something that had been there all along. It was clearly a treasure, buried in the dark earth of time. Here I was, an American named Wallace, hungry for history, especially the stories of heroes and rebellions in the fight to be free. Here I was, and I had never heard of William Wallace.

How could this be? How could the story of Scotland's greatest hero remain untold and unknown to someone like me?

And what the Black Watch guard had told me about what would never be known for sure—what only the legends said about Robert the Bruce and his possible involvement in the betrayal of William Wallace—I knew none of the details of such legends, and yet the first hint of their echo in my life struck me as if I'd been told that Judas Iscariot and Simon Peter were the same individual.

I began instantly to wonder, *What if there was something in the life and death of William Wallace that had the power to transform Robert the Bruce from a plotting, cowardly betrayer to the greatest king in his country's history?*

THE POWER TO TRANSFORM

For as long as I could remember, I had been fascinated by the question of meaningful change in any human's life. Here was a story that encompassed the most profound Transformation. One man, Robert the Bruce, was born to be a king, but he didn't know what a true king really was. A man born a commoner, William Wallace, was the one who showed him how to become not just a king but a great one.

I had found a story. But it would be many years before I had the courage, and the skill, and the desperation to sit down and write it.

The title *Braveheart* was ten years away, and even then it did not occur to me as the name I'd give to William Wallace's story until I was halfway through writing it.

But the question arose: *What does it mean to live with a Braveheart?* That question had led me through life like a ghost carrying a candle through catacombs, leading me toward Heaven, or Hell.

TWO

The Father

The story begins when the Father dies.

From the moment I had first learned of William Wallace, I'd carried the sense that it was a tale full of depth and meaning for me and that I would have to grow in order to tell it. By the time I did sit down to attempt it—understanding that it would be a win-or-die attempt, like an assault onto an enemy's beach—I had been a professional writer for more than a decade.

All the craftsmanship I had acquired in that time told me that the story should begin with William Wallace as an adult. But in the early stages of my striving to live a Braveheart Life, I had learned something vital already:

ALWAYS BEWARE THE WORD *SHOULD*.

I was spared the first *should* by circumstances. There is a cliché of writing instruction that says, "Write what you know." I wanted to write about William Wallace and quickly discovered that almost nothing that could be considered a proven fact was known about him. The *Encyclopedia Britannica*'s entry on him was tiny, and even in the sparse mention the authors of the encyclopedia used vague phrases, such as "born in or around" and "possibly." Years later I would discover that Winston Churchill had mentioned William Wallace in his *History of the English-Speaking Peoples*, and there he declared that almost nothing is known of William Wallace, and yet the legends of his life have inspired the Scottish people for centuries.

Since there were no accepted historical facts to fall back on, I was freed from the notion that research into such facts—which are, in fact, a historian's own perceptions of what is significant—is required to yield a true story. I decided to tell the story that was true for me.

The codes of narrative writing I'd learned from many teachers told me to avoid a slow beginning, or one that would contain characters who weren't directly a part of the main plot. I knew that a movie about William Wallace would require a famous actor to play him, and I anticipated that any large chunk of story that had a child portraying the future hero would end up deleted.

But the legends said that William Wallace's father and brother had died fighting for Scottish independence, and that aspect of his life— for reasons I'm only now beginning to examine—struck me as worth exploring. And after years of waiting, like a man staring at a wide body of water he knows he must someday try to swim across, I had decided to wade in—but I started timidly, at what I first thought was the shallow end.

In my first day of writing, trying to follow what I took to be the broad outlines of William Wallace's life, I came to the point when his father and brother are brought home by their neighbors, dead.

My heart broke for the boy who faced that situation.

YOUNG WILLIAM WALLACE STANDS ALONE AT THE FRESH graves of his father and brother. His mother, long dead, lies in the same ground where the new graves are. A priest intones a burial chant in a language the boy does not understand. He is surrounded by neighbors, none of whom know how to ease the boy's grief. He is utterly Alone.

The adults around him know that if they move to the boy with any gesture of comfort, they will be obliged to take possession of him, so none of them move. Another boy, his best friend, tries to help but has no words.

It is a girl, even younger than young William, who finds his isolation unbearable. She picks a wildflower and carries it back to him. Then she, too, leaves him to his loneliness and grief.

Suddenly a rider appears: a powerful figure full of commitment and purpose, riding in on a white horse. He dismounts and strides straight to the boy. "I'm your Uncle Argyle," he says. His strong hand reaches out to lift the boy's chin so he can study his face and stare into his eyes. "You have the look of your mother."

That night the boy sits beside the hearth with his uncle, in the same small house where young William last heard his father planning the raid that would take his life. "We'll leave tomorrow," Argyle says.

"I don't want to go," the boy says.

"You didn't want your father to die either, did ya?" Argyle says, sharply. "But it happened." And though his last comment has seemed heartless, his next question is reverent. "Did the priest give the benediction?"

"It was in Latin," the boy responds.

"And you don't speak Latin? We shall have to remedy that."

When the boy has gone to bed, his uncle kneels beside the fire and says the prayer of benediction for his brother and nephew. He prays the words from the depth of his heart.

The boy wakes, hearing the wailing of bagpipes. He rises and moves outside the house, where he finds Uncle Argyle staring at the Highlanders who fought beside his father, standing on the hillside. "What are they doing?" the boy asks his uncle.

"Saying good-bye in their own way, playing outlawed tunes on outlawed pipes." He pauses and then tells the boy, "It was the same for me and your dad, when our father was killed."

Now the boy understands far more than he ever grasped before. He sees the sword in his uncle's hand and reaches for it. His uncle lets him hold it and feel its weight—but only for a moment. He takes the sword back and looks into the boy's eyes.

"First, learn to use this," he says, and pokes the boy sharply on his head. "And then I'll teach ya to use this." And he lifts the sword.

THE SWORD

While in college I became captivated by the study of martial arts, especially karate. There are many approaches to unarmed self-defense. Some are called hard and focus on direct attacks, using force against force. Others are called soft and are indirect, using brushing maneuvers to redirect an attacker's assault into a harmless direction. Still other styles of fighting employ dodges and feints to try to completely avoid a clash of blows.

My favorite style drew from all of these. It was called Goju-Shorei and was a blending of hard and soft. The forward hand and arm nearest the opponent was called the Shield; the hand and arm held behind the Shield were thought of as the Sword.

Everyone, it seems to me, must find a Shield and a Sword—one that protects us and one that enables us to penetrate the obstacles we encounter throughout life.

I believe we find the Sword first; a baby's cry is an enormously effective tool for gaining the attention and sustenance it needs to survive and grow. But finding your true Sword is the first step into adulthood.

Using that Sword requires some mastery of the mind. But as martial artists have taught for centuries, it also requires a maturing in the spiritual aspects of life. We must find the Shield too.

And, ultimately, we must learn to use them both together.

William Wallace—at least the one I imagined in *Braveheart*—not only learned a mastery of both weapons but also learned when to lay them both down.

How to do that is a central pillar of the Braveheart Life.

THE WOUND

Just as every Warrior has a Sword, every Warrior has a wound. It may be open, still bleeding beneath his armor, or it may have closed and scarred over—but he remembers it, and it shapes him.

When I was eleven years old, my Father—brilliant, charismatic, loved by all, and loving everyone he knew—began to discover his own great wound. The wound that staggered him, and then brought him to his knees, was mysterious to all of us who loved him, perhaps even to my Father himself. It was as if the champion who led us was suddenly pierced by an archer that none of us, not even he, could see. A man I knew, *knew* to be fearless and resilient and endlessly optimistic became utterly broken. He lost all confidence in himself. He sat and trembled, and wept. He became unable to make a decision or do anything that might help him rise from the pit of despair he had fallen into.

That was a half century ago, and it is only now, as I have written the last paragraph, that I realize my Father's Sword was his confidence; that was the weapon he had used all his life to battle a world that was hostile to him. Without his weapon he was lost and terrified.

And while it was a half century ago, I also realize now that his wound became my wound too. His world fell apart, and so did mine, and the world of our whole family.

But I have come to realize, over my years of struggling and striving to live a Braveheart Life, that our wounds are just as important as our weapons. I suspect we experience our wounds before we choose our weapons, the ones we hope will protect us from further hurt. Yet sometimes even our own weapons cut us.

My Father's wounds, and mine, became just as vital to the creation of *Braveheart*, the story, as they have been to a Braveheart Life.

I believe that if you did not have a wound you would not be reading these pages. By the time you are finished reading them, I hope what I have just written makes sense to you.

THREE

The Men—and the Women— Who Made My Father a Man

When I was a boy and my Father was a young man, he told me many tales. But later the stories matured. They grew deeper, as I grew.

Many of the stories were about Jake Rhodes, the man Thurman called Grandpa. Grandpa Rhodes raised Thurman Wallace, the way Argyle reared William Wallace.

Jake Rhodes loved music and was a prodigious fiddle player. A prodigious father too—he and his wife, Molly, had nine children and raised Thurman as the tenth. Everything about Grandpa Rhodes's life seemed epic. Once he was using a team of mules to pull a mowing machine through a hayfield, and a snake spooked the mules and caused them to bolt. Jake ran to catch them and slipped in the furrows; his foot went under the blades. His foot was severed, all but the Achilles tendon.

The doctor in the nearest town came out to the farm, had Jake placed on the dining room table, gave him whiskey as a sedative, and sewed the foot back on. And it worked. Grandpa limped for the rest of his life, but the doctor saved his foot.

My Father would enthrall me with tales from his own boyhood. I'd beg at bedtime to hear them repeated. Most were funny and involved misadventures—tires falling off trucks or fenders knocked off old cars passing each other on narrow bridges. The Rhodes family inhabited a place known to the locals as Lizard Lick, and my Father saw the humor in this; he saw humor in most everything. One of the first things my Father taught me was how to laugh.

Though I had no consciousness of it at the time, and maybe he didn't either, he was doing more than lifting me into the happiness of humor; he was conveying values, showing me follies that were best laughed at.

And he was transmitting more than that; he was giving me the deeper example of courage. His tales were set in times of poverty and pain, of death and the Great Depression. And all his early examples of how such challenges could be met involved laughter.

In my Father's childhood there seemed little to have laughed at.

Thurman was a scholarly boy, which would not be surprising since his mother went back to school after her husband died and became the teacher at Lizard Lick's one-room schoolhouse, where she taught thirty children at once, spread across eight different grade levels. Her task was complicated by the fact that most of the children were related—to each other and to her.

So Lena did not spare the rod. She used it frequently.

And before she would spank any child for any transgression, she would first paddle my Father.

It took me several years to get my mind around this. My Father mentioned it only in passing, and it was quite a while before its full meaning sank in for me.

What I always understood was that Thurman's grandfather was a man he deeply loved and admired. When he spoke of Grandpa Rhodes, his language was as if he were recounting a parable of the New Testament.

"Once, I was going into town on a Saturday afternoon," my Father said, "for the first time when I could go alone. And Grandpa leaned down and took me by the shoulder and said, 'I'm not a rich man. But you can walk into town and buy anything there if you tell 'em you're my grandson. That's what our name means.'"

MY FATHER WAS NOT AN ESPECIALLY ATHLETIC YOUNG MAN. He was, like his mother, quite nearsighted and had to wear thick glasses. And when he was small, he fell from a tree and shattered his elbow, so his left arm wouldn't straighten.

But there was nothing in the world he wouldn't try. As one of his cousins told me long after he passed away, "Thurman always had that sparkle." He went to work full-time at fourteen, though he stayed in high school. He graduated four years later and just missed being valedictorian; that honor went to Evelyn Page, a sixteen-year-old girl who was so smart she had skipped two grades along her academic way.

She was my Mother.

Thurman and Evelyn had seen each other in high school but had never spoken; she was the quiet girl so much younger than all the others, and he was the leader of everything. They began to get to know each other just before World War II began. Thurman was called up by the draft board and went to basic training, but they sent him home when they discovered that along with being severely nearsighted and having a crooked arm, he was severely short-winded, a condition not aided by the fact that he'd begun rolling his own cigarettes when he was a boy. Thurman went back to Lexington, married Evelyn, and began to work two jobs.

Evelyn was hired as a legal secretary. Everyone in town wanted to hire her; she was brilliant and beautiful. I say this with pride, but the pictures and facts bear me out. From the day a young lawyer hired her to run his office, his practice began to grow. She dreamed of becoming a lawyer herself. She also had dreams of becoming a writer, but that was something she never mentioned until long after I had become one myself.

THEY SAY A FATHER'S DUTY IS TO SAVE THE CHILD FROM THE mother—or at least to help him separate. I don't know if this is true. Surely the child must learn to move away from the identity of both father *and* mother in order to become an adult.

But the hopes and fears of our parents shape us. My parents feared poverty; they had grown up during the Depression. They also feared ignorance. And both of them believed that if only they had gone to college, life would have been far better.

Education became everything. They were fiercely determined to give their children the opportunities they had never known, and they were prepared to sacrifice anything they wanted for themselves to give their children the chance to walk the mysterious corridors of higher education.

And yet they taught me so much that occurred outside of a classroom.

The lessons the Teacher teaches are seldom the ones the Teacher thinks the student is learning.

I did not want to be a scholar. I wanted to be a Warrior.

I thought my Father was not a Warrior. How wrong I would prove to be.

FOUR

A CALLING

MY FATHER DID NOT WANT ME TO BE A WRITER. HE WAS A salesman himself, and it was a wonder to watch him work. With no living father to help him on his way, he had gone to work at fourteen, with such a knack for making friends and relating to people that he could get a job selling almost anything. He forged and sharpened other skills—the weapons of his craft—that made him great as a salesman. He was fiercely optimistic and resilient; he fought against personalizing rejection.

He had learned to ignore his wounds; he'd had a great deal of practice when his mother would spank him before she punished any other students. She would do this even though he was utterly innocent of whatever the others had done. She may have done it because he was innocent, and all his fellow students knew it. Perhaps his mother—a solitary woman with a solitary child, a young woman struggling to succeed in the only job she could find during the Great Depression—was terrified of any reproach, of any accusation of favoritism. Maybe the pain of losing the husband she loved with such youthful passion tainted her natural compassion for her own son. I never knew. I don't think my Father did either. Whatever the reasons, she treated him with anything but justice.

My Father kept this fact from me for many years, not wanting to taint my memories of his mother. When he told me, I asked if he'd ever protested. It seemed difficult for him to confess that, once or twice, he had said, "But I wasn't doing anything," to which his mother replied, "You were instigating it." It would be years before I would understand how this experience in my Father's life had sown the seeds of a collapse of his spirit. But that collapse would come much later in his life.

He was president of his class in high school and captain of the glee club. He even formed a vocal quartet that went around the countryside "barnstorming," singing wherever anyone would pay them.

But one of the more mysterious and wonderful stories about my Father's youth involved a young man of color who lived near my Father's family. This young man—my Father called him a colored fellow when he told me the story—came to young Thurman and told him there were boxing matches being held at the armory in town. He wanted to fight in one of these contests, and he asked my Father to be his manager—to go in and represent him and look after him.

When Daddy told me the story, it was just another tale to him—a lark, an adventure. Now, my Father could speak with the precision and diction of a schoolmarm's son, but when he told tales of Lizard Lick, he lapsed into a buzz saw of an accent that sang with music and color.

"We drove into town all together, me and my friends with the boxer, and we were all there to cheer him on. And he got in the fight, and he got to doing pretty good. And then he got to doing *real* good! He got to doing so good that he started looking at us and laughing and really enjoying it all! And that was when the other feller caught him a good one. And ya know," Daddy said, pausing to grin at the memory, "we were halfway back to the Lick before he woke up good."

I wanted to hear more details of that event, but none were forthcoming. My Mother would shoot a look at Daddy whenever he ventured into story territory that might touch on subjects she preferred to keep buried, and this story fell into that kind of vault. But what intrigued me then—and has whispered to my consciousness even more as time goes on—was what kind of presence my Father must have had, not just in his school but in his community, that a young black man, living in the state that gave birth to the Ku Klux Klan, would come to my Father and trust him to be the one who would speak for him, negotiate for him, look out for him in the rough-and-tumble world of boxing in the local armory in the dark days before World War II.

Daddy, as I have said, wasn't an athlete.

But he was afraid of exactly nothing.

A time would come when it seemed my Father was afraid of everything.

I would come to that time in my own life.

When it happened to my Father, I thought it was the worst time I would ever experience. When it happened to me, I thought that time was even worse.

From both of them, *Braveheart* was born.

⟨⟨⟨◦⟩⟩⟩

I REALIZED EARLY ON THAT MY FATHER WANTED ME TO BE A candy salesman, just as he had become. He wanted to build a family business. He wanted to teach his son everything he knew.

I loved sports; my Father did not. If you tossed a ball to Daddy, it would hit him in the nose, if not on his horn-rim glasses. I loved to run, and he couldn't keep up from the time I was seven. I was desperate to learn to swim, especially underwater—to me, it was like flying. When he was in a lake or a pool, what he called swimming was a stroke like a drowning spaniel. After ten feet of dog paddling, he'd stand up proudly and declare he'd had a fine workout.

There was one other thing I loved as much as running and wrestling and banging heads with other boys: making up stories. Early on I became aware that when I stopped and stared—at a forest or into an aquarium or into the clouds when I was lying on grass—stories began to form in my head.

These stories were linked to emotion and stimulated by music. If I heard a stirring song, such as "The Battle Hymn of the Republic" or "Dixie," I would imagine great battles.

My Mother's mother, Grandmother Page, had a country store. It was built of a single room, with a potbellied stove in the center. Farmers gathered in front of that stove and sat on nail kegs and talked. On the back side of the store were stacks of pig and chicken feed sacks. One day I fashioned a desk out of those sacks of feed, and there I wrote my first story, of brave men and battles with rascals on the Tennessee River and in the woods surrounding it.

Strange—or not strange at all—that I can sit beside a hearth a half century later (as I am sitting at the fireplace of my new home as I write these words) and can still smell the oiled wood floor of my Grandmother's country store and the fragrance of the feed. I can still feel the texture of the sacks and the roughness of the paper on the writing pad as the smooth point of my pencil fashioned words that came to me from . . . *Somewhere.* There are Moments in our lives we do not forget.

From that time forward I was on a journey. It began long before then, but that was when I began to be aware of it. When teachers would announce that the classroom assignment was to write a story, and my schoolmates would groan, I found myself eager, even excited. When I read great writing, like that of Twain or Dickens, it thrilled me. I had no concept of doing it professionally. I did it because it was joy.

My parents sacrificed to save the money so my sister and I could go to college—something my parents had desperately wanted for themselves but had never been able to do. When the time came for me to go, I chose the most expensive place of all my options, Duke University, and my Father was deeply proud of my choice.

I wrote when I was there, and I also wrote songs, a practice I'd begun in high school when I realized that much of my favorite music had been created by the same people who were singing it. In college I even started a little record company, and I wrote, sang, produced, and sold my own records. I made it onto the record charts in a couple of small towns. I didn't make a living at it, but I was certainly living.

For my Father and, therefore, for me, making a living was what a man had to do.

The question became for me, how can I make a living and still be living?

Another unforgettable moment in my life happened on a run I took with the man I grew up with and have always considered my Brother, James Connor. (I've always called him "Diamond," short for "Diamond Jim," though he is as far from glitz as a man can be. I think the name stuck because of the strength and purity of his heart.) We were on a running trail in our hometown, Lynchburg, Virginia, where our family had moved when I was twelve after my Father had changed jobs. We were nearing graduation from college, and both of us were wondering what our professions might be. I told him I was utterly in the dark about it. After four years of studying religion, Russian, creative writing, and all sorts of other liberal arts courses, I had no idea.

And Diamond said something that hit me like a breath from Heaven: "Gee, Buzz" [his name for me—another story I won't tell], "I always thought you'd be a writer."

FIVE

A Calling—and a Piano-Playing Pig

But neither my Moments writing on the pig-feed desk in my Grandmother's store or walking with Diamond Jim gave me enough light to see into the darkness of my future.

In college I was drawn to the formal study of Religion. People I meet now seem baffled, even dismayed, when I tell them this, due to the prejudices of the age in which we live and the assumed connections between dogma and intolerance. Most of us don't bother to distinguish between Faith and fanaticism. Modern people will say, "I'm spiritual but not religious." I know what they're trying to convey is that they don't look down on others because of their beliefs. Of course, quite often this is utterly false; they *do* look down on others for *precisely* that reason, for having a belief they do not share.

The implication is that any belief is a bad one; any belief that causes a person to change direction, make any real alteration in life, undergo any transformation, change any value system is bad. I say that is the only belief that *is* a belief. If you truly believe something, then it must truly change you.

When I was at the university, I realized that the exploration of such questions was the most compelling path of study for me, and I chose to major in religion. Because I did, others began to assume that I was intending to become a professional pastor, and I began to wonder about that myself.

I felt a sense of the profound value of the people in such a profession. People whom I deeply admired were in it. One of them was the pastor of my home church. His name was Albert E. Simms. He was a majestic man—wise, eloquent, brimming with brains and talent and tenderness, and humble too. He never wanted to be called Reverend, just Mr. Simms.

When I was home one summer I went to see him in his office at our church. I sat down across from him at his desk, and he asked me plainly, "Do you feel the calling to be a pastor?"

I was on the spot; he had asked me so simply, and I could only answer as honestly as I knew how. "No, sir," I said, "I really don't feel it. But I know it's the greatest calling anyone could have."

"You're wrong," Mr. Simms said. "The greatest calling is the one God has for you."

⊗⊘⊗⊘⊗

DIAMOND JIM, A VORACIOUS READER, HAD TOLD ME OF JOSEPH Campbell's advice that we follow our bliss.[1] Such was the feeling I experienced in writing, especially in the creation of songs. I had already begun to muse about a career in music when I heard that Kris Kristofferson, whose writing I found magnificent, was coming to my university to perform.

A buddy of mine in the Religion Department was on the student committee that hosted the concert, and he arranged to get me backstage before the performance began. I was thrilled. Kris Kristofferson, to me, was, and is, a titan. A poet, a Rhodes scholar, a boxer, a US Army Ranger, an artist whose work deals with the longing for faith, family, and courage. I took him to be an artist I might emulate.

My friend led me across the cables and chaos behind the curtained stage, and suddenly I found myself in front of a tall, bearded man with bright—and somewhat bloodshot—eyes. I introduced myself. He looked me in the eye, smiled, and shook my hand with quick strength. I blurted something along the lines that I wanted to write as he did and had thought of going to Nashville. I don't remember my words, but I remember his precisely. He said, "Aw, man! You gotta go!"

He did not seem totally sober when he said it.

But what genius ever seems totally sober? And isn't a drunk genius still a genius?

BECAUSE I'D EXPERIENCED SO MUCH EXCITEMENT IN MUSIC, and I wanted to follow my bliss—and felt encouraged by my chance meeting with Kris Kristofferson, whose writing I so admired—I felt the time had come for me to take the plunge.

I had begun graduate work at Duke Divinity School, studying alongside young men and women who were committed seminarians. When I decided to leave school, I felt a deep guilt. Part of it was connected to my parents' ambitions for me; they wanted me to go into one of the professions that schooling enabled, such as medicine or law. Songwriter was not one of those professions. But I also felt a sense of shame in leaving my classmates who were destined to become pastors themselves.

One of them, when I told him of my inner conflict, said, "If I could do what you do, I'd do it." His name was Andrew; I named my first son after him. I felt so selfish leaving the young men and women who were going to hold the hands of the dying and help the hungry to grow food and clothe the homeless. Andrew gave me something: he fed the hungry in me.

I went to Nashville and found a job at a new theme park that was about to open there; it was called Opryland and was imagined as a sort of musical Disney World. I auditioned as a singer/songwriter. When I finished singing, the lead judge asked me, "Are you afraid of animals?"

The job title was Manager of Animal Shows. I was given the task of creating a show that featured barnyard animals that were trained to play musical instruments. I am not making this up.

We had a pig who played the piano and a duck who played a drum. I put a sequined bowtie on the pig and named him Pigerace, after pianist Liberace. I dubbed the duck Burt Bachaquack.

Imagine how proud my parents were.

During that time, I worked eighty to a hundred hours a week. To be able to write songs and still manage Burt and Pigerace, I would get up at four thirty every morning and work for a while before I'd go to the barn to get my performers ready. (You may laugh, and I hope you do, but it was perfect training for becoming a movie director!)

After being in Nashville for about a year, I landed a contract with Tree Music, Nashville's most powerful music publisher at the time, to write songs.

But I had no hit songs in Nashville. Maybe it was the music business then, or maybe it was me. I felt crushed, even hopeless.

I went to California. At least there the sun was shining.

A year later I met a woman, the one I would marry. The first time I went to her apartment I found something on her coffee table; it was a screenplay written by her father, Jim Cullen, a man who would become a second father to me. I picked it up and looked inside it. And my life changed.

⁂

I HAVE SAID THERE ARE MOMENTS IN OUR LIVES THAT WE DO not forget, the kind of luminous moments when we find ourselves standing on a mountaintop—the way William Wallace stood on a peak in the Highlands when all that he had known before had changed and all that he might become stretched before him—and we see our lives in a different way.

Those Moments make a movie. Those Moments make a life.

What makes a Moment?

Before we move forward in the adventure of exploring that question, I want to tell you about another man I know, someone who grew up seemingly as far from Tennessee as possible on planet Earth. I say seemingly because I have been astonished at how closely our hearts, minds, and values align, how much a sense of humor we share, and how extraordinary he is as a Friend.

His life was shaped by a different kind of father—and a special mother too.

And I think it's important for me to tell you a bit of his story at this point in our talk of Freedom and the Braveheart Life, lest I seem to imply that you must have a background like mine in order to live it.

SIX

BOB FROM AFGHANISTAN

IN THE EARLY PART OF THE TWENTIETH CENTURY, A NEW king of Afghanistan, whose father had been assassinated after he had fought his way back into power following a bloody conspiracy, wanted to solidify his royal authority over the Kandahar region. Kandahar was then, as it is now, controlled by independent leaders who were unconquerable. The young king saw that it was crucial for him to find some way to bring the tribesmen there under the rule of the crown.

The king had a friend, a man so loyal and brave he had fought for the king and had taken a bullet in the fight to restore the monarchy. This friend was allowed to marry the king's aunt—one of many wives— and the king declared him the new governor and sent him to Kandahar. Even Alexander the Great with an utterly ruthless army had been frustrated in his efforts to bring the Pashtuns of Kandahar to heel. And this new governor was no fool.

When the governor arrived in Kandahar, he immediately set out to forge a relationship with the man who was the most feared and thus the most powerful tribal leader of the entire Helmand province. All the tribes there considered him to be the real Head Man. The governor knew he must meet the tribal leader face to face. And both of them knew that the other man wielded great power. They lived in a world where ambushes and other forms of assassination were common political tools; neither of them was a stranger to any form of killing. They knew there was a risk in meeting; they knew there was a risk in not meeting. They needed each other. So the governor and the tribesman sat down together—and a strange thing happened.

They became friends.

They discovered they both loved to play chess. So they began to play. They were in the middle of a game when the governor looked across the board at the tribal leader and asked, "Do you have a favorite son?"

The tribal leader stared across at the man he considered a visitor to his domain. He knew this governor, with the backing of the king, could summon an army of greater numbers with more plentiful, modern weapons and more ammunition than the Kandahar tribesmen could muster, but the Pashtuns of Kandahar and Helmand would fight over anything. They believed, in fact, that the sole purpose of a man was to prove his manhood wherever possible through his willingness to fight. The tribal leader could see this new governor had a wisdom about him and a directness that came with bravery.

"Yes," the tribal leader answered, "I have a favorite son."

"If he is your favorite," the governor said, "he must be strong. And brave."

The tribal leader recognized the compliment but saw there was more to this than flattery. "He is both," the Head Man of Kandahar said. "Like you, like the king, I am respected, and I have authority, but there are still times when there is trouble. Whatever trouble happens in the future, I know my strongest son will handle it."

The governor nodded. In that moment he seemed to make up his mind about something. "I have a favorite daughter," he said. "She is tall and beautiful, and she is brilliant too. She speaks both languages of our people. She respects our faith. And though she is elegant and would bring grace to the grandest event in Kabul, she never fails to remember the beggars in the streets."

Now the tribesman understood, but it was not his place to make the offer. He waited for the governor to continue. "We can fight each other forever," he said. "Or your son and my daughter can marry, and then everything good that happens, not just in Kandahar and Helmand but in all of Afghanistan, will be good for both our families."

They agreed.

The governor returned to Kabul and informed his daughter of his arrangement. She was fourteen years old.

She was not happy with this news. She was the opposite. She told her father, "I will kill myself before I marry an animal like the son of this tribesman of Kandahar."

"Then kill yourself," the governor told his daughter. "It is either that or marry him because the arrangement is made."

The beautiful and intelligent girl did not kill herself. It can't be said that she agreed since her opinion was never considered in the matter. She went to Kandahar, and she became the first wife of the man who himself would come to be the most influential tribal leader of the entire Helmand province.

That tribesman and his young wife were the mother and father of my Friend: Bob from Afghanistan.

I MET HIM IN SHERMAN OAKS IN A RESTAURANT ON VENTURA Boulevard. I saw him many times before we ever spoke. The restaurant was a cheerful, cozy place with great food and waiters and waitresses who were full of fun. It was my kind of place, and his too. Both of us went several times a week for breakfast, sometimes to meet friends and sometimes alone. I'd often see a man there, sitting thoughtfully and quietly. There was something different about him; he had high cheek-bones and straight, jet-black hair. He was compact, broad shouldered, and small waisted. He walked like an athlete and even sat like one. I couldn't place his ethnicity; he struck me somehow as European or perhaps Middle Eastern, but his clothes were definitely Italian. Gucci, Armani—in brighter colors than I'd ever seen any other guy able to pull off, but the blues and greens and purples looked elegant on him. He always wore a sport coat, immaculately tailored. I thought he had to be some kind of Eurotrash Lounge Lizard.

We met because of a Porsche. Specifically, two Porsches. I know what you're thinking: anybody who owns a Porsche is a Lizard—and maybe you're right. But whenever he twists that key on the left side of the dashboard and hears that engine behind him roar to life, he is one happy Lizard.

I have a primal love of cars, the same love that made some hill-billies run moonshine even when they didn't care to drink it. There's just nothing like the sound and the surge and the swaying, not to mention the smell. Every man who loves cars knows the smell of smoking tires and hot brakes and the countryside rushing past an open window.

When I was a boy, my Father bought us a house in a row of brick homes in a Memphis neighborhood that had been cotton fields until the GIs flooded back from World War II. In the evenings the neighbors would gather in the front yards, sitting in lawn chairs and watching their Baby Boomer children play. One of those evenings I crawled onto my Father's lap. "Daddy," I said, "David Lee has a new bicycle."

"I saw that," Daddy said.

"Ronnie has one too," I said.

"Yeah! Red one. Nice," he said.

"I want one too," I told him.

He reached into his pocket and pulled out a quarter. "You cut the grass this morning," he said. "Here's your pay."

I had sufficient math skills to do some calculations. "But . . ." I protested. "But . . . a bicycle costs . . . a lot! I'll be old before I can save up enough to get one!"

"The neighbors have grass," he said.

I understood, even at six years old, that he expected me not only to work but also to go out and get the work.

Looking back on it now, I understand why he was so troubled to the point of sickness when I decided to try my hand at songwriting. It didn't strike him as enterprising or hardworking or wise.

Something his training did do for me, though, was make me appreciate owning things I'd earned by my own work.

Which leads us back to the Porsche.

When I began to write full-time for television, my income began to soar. In my first year my income doubled—then redoubled, then *re*doubled, then *redoubled*. For the first time in my life, I was awash in money. I bought a new house, a big car for my wife and children, insurance policies, investment accounts. And I still had money.

The people I worked around had fancy cars. My boss had a Ferrari Testarossa, and he'd spent an additional fortune having the car turned into a convertible. All of this is my rationalization.

I bought the car I'd always wanted: a 911 Porsche. Red. Bright red. My writer friend Jack Bernstein, who would go on to write *Ace Ventura: Pet Detective*, said it could be seen from Mars.

I was careful where I parked it; for a while I was edgy about driving it anywhere. But I drove to my breakfast place, hoping to get a spot at one of the parking meters in front of the restaurant so nobody would open a door on my car, as they might if I had to park in a lot.

I drove up. And there in front of the restaurant sat another brand-new 911—only this one a convertible, more expensive and elegant than the one I'd just bought.

I parked directly behind it, got out, and stared at the other car, in full view of the other customers and the waiters and waitresses who all knew me. I walked into the restaurant and saw them all laughing.

I called out, "*Who* is the guy who won't let me have the cool new car for *one day* before he buys a better one?!"

And the guy in the Armani sport coat and Gucci glasses lifted his hand and waved me over. "Sit!" he said with a smile. "I buy you breakfast!"

I sat down, and we both were laughing. "I'm Randy," I said.

"Robert," he said, offering me his hand. "Call me Bob."

His given name, I would learn later, was something Americans had trouble remembering and pronouncing, but everybody could remember Bob. He was raised in the wild lands of Afghanistan on the high plains beneath the Hindu Kush.

But his heart was born in America.

⚬⚬⚬⚬⚬

BOB ONCE TOLD ME A STORY. HE WAS ONE OF MANY BROTH-ers, born somewhere in the middle of the pack. His people did not mark birthdays the way we do. One brother was called Favorite; he was neither the eldest nor the youngest of the sons. He was simply his father's favorite. At festivals and other holidays, whenever gifts were given out, he got the biggest and finest. No one minded this, Bob told me; it was the way of things.

This brother adored and admired their father, and later in his life, after the father's death, he even changed his name so that he would be called as his father had been.

Bob, however, detested his father and refused to ever call his brother by their father's name. Bob took exception to the way his father had treated his mother. This did not keep Bob and his brother from loving each other and delighting in their shared company. They could compartmentalize feelings, even deep ones, and keep them from disrupting their common bond.

All of Bob's siblings had striking talents and abilities. Two were champion athletes—Bob was a master of strength events—and

38

they went on to distinguished careers. His elder brother became a high-ranking police official in Kabul; another brother became a distinguished mathematician.

Bob was officially not the favorite, but something about him struck his father as special. How do I know? By a story he told me.

In Kabul, they lived in a modest home near his mother's relatives, for his grandfather did not believe in displaying wealth or influence. But out in the Helmand province, where his father held sway, things were different. They owned thousands of acres of land. Their home was large, but it lacked amenities, such as air conditioning and flush toilets. (Maybe that was a shared bond between Bob from Afghanistan and me from Tennessee; we'd both lived in places that used outhouses.) In the summer it was too hot to sleep in their normal bedrooms, so all the boys would climb onto the flat roof and lie down on blankets beneath the stars. Afghanistan sits at an altitude with thinner air, and the stars were brilliant.

A storyteller would come visit each night, and he would sit down and recite an epic story, completely from memory. As he spoke, he'd watch the boys as they drifted off to sleep. The next night he would resume the story at the exact place where the first boy had begun to slumber, so no one missed anything.

When Bob was telling me this, I was enthralled up to this point. Bob himself is a fascinating storyteller. His vocabulary in English— one of the many languages he speaks fluently—is greater than mine, with one particular omission: he never uses the articles *a*, *an*, or *the*. Couple that with the slight accent he carries and the tonal variations in his speech, which are absolutely musical, and he is captivating. The descriptions of brothers lying together beneath the stars in the foothills of the Hindu Kush, leading all the way to Mount Everest at the very top of the world, had brought me to a poetic reverence.

But that was just setting the stage for the real story to begin.

"So my father," Bob told me, "shook me awake one night when my brothers were all sleeping, and the storyteller was gone. Father said, 'Come with me.' His voice was quiet, he wanted me not to wake others, so I follow him to other side of roof.

"I whispered, 'What is it?' and he made signal for me to be still, just wait. So I sit with my father. It is long time to me. And then, suddenly, over the wall climbs . . . Abrahim!"

He said the name with a breathlessness that testified to the awe he still felt for that moment.

"Now, Beeg Guy"—Bob's accent is impossible for me to describe. I love it, and I can't render it, except to say that Big Guy sounds like "Beeg Guy"; it's my nickname from Bob, and I'm as proud of it as I am of any moniker I have from any friend—"I tell you who Abrahim is. In Helmand province he is boogeyman! He is bandit, so famous that mothers threaten their children that if they don't behave, she will tell Abrahim to come get them! Afghans—and the Pashtun, my tribe—will fight anybody in world, but if Abrahim stops convoy and says, 'I am robbing you!' then *nobody* reaches for weapon. Shoot at Abrahim, they say, and he will come kill you, your children, your friends, your cattle, *everything*!

"Man leaps over wall, in moonlight! He is over six feet tall! He has long mustache, rifle, ammunition belts crossing his chest. I whisper 'Abrahim!' and my father looks at me once, his eyes say, 'Silent!' Abrahim moves to my father, gets on his knees, and *kisses my father's hand*!

"Beeg Guy, I can't tell you how amazed I am. So amazed I stop trembling. My father points his finger at Abrahim! He says, 'You are my friend, but you have robbed too many trucks, too much. Government wants to punish you, police come to Kandahar, get in way, this is not good.'

"Abrahim listens, he says only, 'What do you want me to do?' My father says, 'You turn yourself in. You go to jail. I take care of your family. You will not stay in jail long—I will get you out.'

"Abrahim nods. Again he kisses my father's hand—then jumps back over the wall, and he is gone!"

There is more to this story. There is more to every story. I will tell you what more of it I know—if you have not yet fallen asleep. If you have, you wouldn't know a great story if it hit you in the face.

But what struck me about the story to this point is how much is already there, and how much has not been said—such as Bob's father knew the notorious and terrifying Abrahim so well that he could arrange a secret meeting with him in the middle of the night. Abrahim humbled himself before Bob's father; he knelt before him; he kissed his hand—and he did what he was told to do.

But most striking of all to me is that Bob's father woke him—him alone, among all his extraordinary brothers—and brought him to that secret meeting.

BEFORE I GO ON, I WANT TO STOP FOR A MOMENT AND SAY something about Brothers, for Brothers—and Sisters too—are essential in the Braveheart Life. My Mother and Father had no other sons, so I have no brother—but I have many Brothers. Well, maybe not many; but if you believe, as I do, that one or two True Friends together is an army, then any number of True Brothers in your Chosen Family is a massive and powerful group. Jesus knew exactly what he was saying when he told his followers, "Where two or more are gathered in my name, there will I be also."[1]

The relationships that William Wallace has with Hamish and Stephen of Ireland in *Braveheart* are certainly two of the most powerful aspects of the story. So let us pause for a moment, stare into the flames of our fire, and talk about Brothers and Sisters.

SEVEN

BROTHERS AND SISTERS

IN *BRAVEHEART* HAMISH IS WILLIAM'S FRIEND, A FRIEND HE has had since childhood. In that way, and in other ways, too, he is most like a birth brother. He and William test their strengths against each other, they compete, and sometimes they even fight. But the fighting has an understanding. An *understanding*—a truth that is *standing under*: they are Friends; they are there for each other. Always.

Stephen of Ireland, on the other hand, enters William's life much later, when he is already a famous warrior. For a lot of men I know, Stephen is their favorite character in *Braveheart*, after William, and I must confess that I relate to him myself with great delight. Stephen's bizarre relationship with God, his talking to God directly in ways that are simultaneously sacred and profane, came from my own life, and his character was also inspired by my wife and her Irish family—a group of people so full of fire and creativity and wit and heart, a group I love so much, that such qualities coming out in my writing of a man from Ireland was inevitable.

I love that Stephen is a new friend.

Many years ago, shortly after I had moved to California and began trying to break into the business, someone told me, "When a man becomes a star, the only friends he has are old friends and other stars."

This, even then, seemed to me to be a sad and lonely state of affairs. I understood it to mean that for anyone with celebrity, the trust required for True Friendship meant it became more and more rare.

When Stephen of Ireland meets William Wallace, William is already a notorious rebel leader, and Stephen is unknown to all the Scots. But Stephen, much to his own delight, as well as to mine, is a legend in his own mind. He is brimming with courage, self-confidence, and self-respect—if not outright self-delusion, which is one of the traits I find most admirable in the Irish. He would die for William, and William would die for him. Who wouldn't want a friend like that?

When William Wallace is dying, Hamish and Stephen are there to be with him.

Others are there too. Murron is there. God is there. But more about that later.

IN HIS BEAUTIFUL BOOK *THE FOUR LOVES*, C. S. LEWIS IDEN-tifies Friendship as the first of the great loves, and he gives us a brilliant insight into its nature. He says that at some point in the history of humanity, Friendship did not exist. Hunters killed animals for food out of the basic need to survive. But then one day, a single hunter realized that a deer was not only tasty but also beautiful, and for a time after that, the hunter was the loneliest man on earth. Then one day he noticed another hunter had paused to stare at the grace and the glory of the deer running through the forest, and in that moment, Friendship was born.

Friends share and embrace what is deepest and truest and most essential about us, and in so doing, they become our True Brothers and Sisters. I realize I've just said that Friendship and True Brotherhood and Sisterhood are the same thing, but I want to sharpen the edge of that statement. We can speak of the brotherhood of all men, but that is an abstract concept. As a goal, we can say that all of us on earth are family. This is something only God can achieve.

Not everyone, even our natural siblings, will see and embrace *who we really are* in the same way our real Friends do. Maybe one of the bravest and best attitudes to take with those who don't accept us as we are—and who can accept us absolutely except God?—is to give them the freedom not to love us as we are.

THIS BRINGS ME BACK TO BOB FROM AFGHANISTAN.

Apparently Bob's father wasn't the only one in the family to recognize his strength as a man. His brothers saw it too. When they were young men, shortly before the Russians invaded their country and turned it upside down, Bob's older brother, the police official, came to Bob and said, "Our youngest brother has allied himself with the communists. He has, in fact, become their leader. I don't care if he believes in Communism, but he is stirring up violence against the king. You tell our brother to stop—or I will have to deal with him."

Bob had a particular affection for his youngest brother; I could see it when he told me this tale. He said his youngest brother was a deep thinker—poetic and caring. From what I can gather, this brother was the one most like Bob among all his other siblings.

Bob went to his youngest brother and told him what their older brother had said. And the youngest brother responded, "Tell him you have told me. And tell him I see the rich people in this country enslaving the poor. Tell him I have sworn to fight for them, and I will never stop. Tell him to do his worst."

The elder brother never jailed his youngest brother or brought any other force against him, though Bob had reported that his diplomatic efforts had not produced agreement. Perhaps the older brother might have attempted something, but when the Russians invaded Afghanistan, all those who had been part of the established government became wanted men, and he was forced to flee his country on foot, climbing across the Himalayas without mountaineering equipment. When he reached safety, all his fingernails had broken off in his journey.

The poetic younger brother, however, did not escape the consequences of his attempt to help his country's downtrodden by leading the underground Communist movement. When the Russians came with their armies and their columns of Stalin tanks, the younger brother saw evil in them, too, and he fought them as furiously as he had fought the previous local government.

There was competition for leadership within the Afghan resistance, even among the cells of various communist groups that wanted power. One day Bob's brother went into a house where he had been led to believe he could obtain weapons to use in fighting the Russians; he was never seen again. The man who had enticed Bob's brother to the house died soon after in a hail of machine gun bullets fired by a man on the back of a motorbike in the streets of Kabul.

When Bob told me this, I felt a grief for his idealistic younger brother, as I could see Bob did when he related this part of the tale. Normally hearing of the death of any communist would not disturb me. I grew up seeing communists as the epitome of those who would take away freedom and would freely use mass murder as a tool for their goals. But this was different.

Bob's story has helped inspire me toward a Braveheart Life. He has shown me how people in an extraordinary yet utterly human situation faced critical situations and responded with massive courage.

That is what any real art does.

Come to think of it, what is the relationship of art and a Braveheart Life? Where does art come from?

Spoiler alert: it comes from Love.

EIGHT

ART AND THE BRAVEHEART LIFE

TOLSTOY ONCE WROTE A STORY ENTITLED "THE WOOD-Felling." In this story, Russians in the late 1800s are fighting tribes in the Caucasus Mountains. The weapons are somewhat different, and the soldiers use horse-drawn carts instead of diesel-powered trucks, but other than that, the situation is not terribly different for them than for Americans in Afghanistan today.

In Tolstoy's story a group of Russians goes out to cut firewood to burn for heat against the constant cold; one of them is shot by a sniper. The man who is shot knows his wound is mortal, and when his comrades place him on the wood cart to transport him back to their camp, he begins to beg the lieutenant in charge of the group to take the letters his wife has sent him and return them to her.

The lieutenant, aged by the war to the point of numbness, says he'll do it, but the dying soldier knows he won't; he's seen too many men pitched into shallow graves by other men who no longer care about anything.

The two men argue for a moment, the lieutenant promising emptily, the dying man growing more agitated and insistent as his death approaches. "The letters are in my boot," he tells the young lieutenant. "Take them! Take them! If you have the letters in your hand, you won't throw them away!"

At last the lieutenant agrees, and he has the dying man's trouser leg cut away, his boot removed, and the layers of cloth he has used to try to stay warm unwrapped to find the letters. But with the letters he discovers something else.

For the first time in months, the young lieutenant sees the bare white flesh of a man's leg, and it is *this* that reminds the young officer that the dying man is a human being. The lieutenant has seen blood and gaping chest wounds and heads blown open, but the naked, tender flesh is what reminds him of the tenderness of life and the tragedy of its senseless loss.

When I first came across this story in college, it struck me even then that I'd suddenly been shown an essential quality of art: *art is the revelation of truth.* Art is not static; it is alive—because we are. As we live, we become used to some things, less sensitive to their power to generate insight and experience. Art must flow, to speak to us as we do.

It is this way with most things human. Styles of language, music, even clothes change so that our senses will be attentive. In one decade the ideal woman is skin and bones. In another she is robust, and in another she is muscled. In the 1940s men fighting a world war listened to smooth saxophones in big bands. Two decades later their children tried to drop out of society with distorted electric guitars as their soundtrack.

So art is not a process of repetition. It can't be created by asking what has worked in the past to hold up—as if anew—the image that will remind us all that we are alive, and human.

That's why I see my Friend Bob's life as a work of art. His personal history—his adventure, his character, the depth of his heart—is all stunning. He is a marvel to me, and a joy. He came to America with no money and a vocabulary of four words: *yes*, *no*, and *apple pie*. He worked three jobs at once while attending community college. There he displayed a remarkable aptitude for numbers. But Bob chose business and specialized in the buying and selling of land. He could evaluate the long-term potential of property simply by finding it on a map. He made a vast fortune, which he has arranged to donate to charity. And all the while he has remained so physically fit that he still resembles the champion athlete he was as a teenager.

He is the epitome of someone who lives with a Braveheart.

And the one in his family whom he most resembles is not his father. It is his mother.

Reflecting on this now brings me to a full stop—one of those moments when truth hits us in a new way and causes us to ponder, just as art does since both are really Truth.

The Truth in this, for me, is that my Father nurtured my growth as a man. My journey as an artist is rooted in my Mother.

There are many oversimplifications of the interplay of the masculine and feminine in our lives. For me, the dynamics of Father and Mother had less to do with their genders than it did with their unique characters. Certainly my Father, the salesman, was an extrovert in the classic male mold; my Mother was reserved and sometimes said that if she had to sell anything to make a living, then we would all starve. But introspection is not the only quality of an artist. In fact, any real artist who sees art not solely as self-expression but, rather, sees it largely as a way of connecting with others will need a salesman's willingness to face rejection.

I want to say, too, that manliness seems to have been de-emphasized and even attacked in the last several decades, but I know of no field where the qualities of what I would call a Braveheart Man would not be valuable.

As I was growing up, if I slammed my head through a window or broke an arm from a disagreement with playground equipment or drove a car at speeds frowned on by the law, my Mother would clearly be in favor of locking me away while my Father would dust me off, give me a nod and a smile, and send me off again. These are not small differences. But the more I see of life, the more I understand that such positions are taken as a team; one parent could take a certain stance precisely because the balancing position was being taken by the other. Both my parents were Parents in full.

Still, there is truth in saying my parents gave me art. When I wrote a poem or a song, and later when I wrote stories, my Father's primary response was practical: What good is this? Can it be sold? Mama's was different; she wondered, what was I really saying? She saw the art.

What hymns were saying, not just in their words but also in the turns and lifts of their music, spoke not just to her ears but to her soul. So did poetry, and that greatest poetry of all, the Bible. She knew what it meant and what it felt like.

I believe it is impossible to overestimate the power a boy feels and the influence it has in his life when he looks at his Mother and sees that she has seen him, has looked into his soul and found something there that makes her glow.

⸙⸙⸙⸙

OF COURSE, THERE IS ANOTHER SIDE OF WOMEN, AND THAT IS the power of their withholding—of attention, approval, affection. It, too, has a profound effect on men. One of those simplistic metaphors about the sexes is that men are the sun, burning full force in the sky every day, while women are the moon, constantly shifting, sometimes shining gloriously and romantically, sometimes disappearing alto- gether. I love the moon; there is a shot of the full moon in almost every movie I've directed. The presence of the moon, especially when it's a full circle, whether hanging in a clear sky or slipping in and out of drift- ing clouds, fills me with a sense of reverence and magic.

Being in love is something like being in that sacred and magical state all the time.

Divorcing is like swallowing a live hand grenade, one that blows your guts all over the place.

I've been there. My wife and I went through it, along with our children and family and friends. Divorce is a dark and savage place. Mine happened several years after *Braveheart*, but I would equate it to the same dismemberment William Wallace experienced.

I have no divorce stories or advice to share, except for one. And it happened on a Father's Day, my first after the marriage ended.

I had spent the morning with my kids, Andrew and Cullen, and all of us had struggled through a brunch, trying to regain a sense of balance and peace. That evening I was on a plane, flying to New York. And on that plane I wrote each of them a letter.

I told them, in the best words I could find, how much I love them. I told them I never wanted them to feel that by loving me they were being disloyal to their mother, or by loving her they were being disloyal to me. I told them that both of us love both of them with all our hearts—I knew that for sure.

But I told them even more. I told them I remembered vividly the day each of them was born and that their mother's courage on those days still filled me with respect and awe. And I told them that so much of what I love about them, traits that are extraordinary and unique, came directly from their mother.

I find this is an aspect of the glorious Grace of children. Two parents who associate each other with joy can come to identify the same relationship with terrible pain, yet their children, who carry so much of both of them, are bearers of their attractive and beautiful qualities.

I sent the letters to my sons. I don't know if their mother ever read them, but I do know that my relationship with her began to heal around that time. The pain began to dim a bit; a hint of joy began to return. We celebrate our sons at every possible chance, and there are many such chances to rejoice and laugh. Now she is marrying a man she loves dearly and with whom she finds great happiness.

God finds ways to penetrate the darkness and ways to Love and Honor that we would never expect.

A man who does not Honor women can never live a Braveheart Life.

51

SPEAKING OF HONORING WOMEN, I WANT TO EMPHASIZE THAT they can be more than encouragers and supporters but can themselves be Warriors, even champions of what I am calling the Braveheart Life.

My Friend Jill Conner Browne comes exploding to mind. (Jill does not simply appear, ever.)

Jill Conner Browne was a young mother without a college education when her husband left her with $50,000 in credit card debt, a baby, and a mother with Alzheimer's disease. Jill was working three jobs, trying to survive, when she was fired from one of them—humor columnist for the local newspaper—because the editor had decided she was "not funny." So in her fleeting (and desperate) free moments, she wrote the first of what became an iconic stream of bestselling books full of heart and humor. Among them are *God Save the Sweet Potato Queens*, *The Sweet Potato Queens' Big-Ass Cookbook (and Financial Planner)*, and *The Sweet Potato Queens' Field Guide to Men: Every Man I Love Is Either Married, Gay, or Dead*.

From the day I met her twelve years ago at a convention—where we both gave speeches and I was good, but she was great—we have scarcely gone twenty-four hours without talking to each other. She's married to one of my finest friends, who proposed to her by assembling all her friends and extended family and getting on his knees in front of her and saying, "I know if I marry you, I'm marrying everybody here, so I'm asking you this way . . ." Talk about a Warrior-Poet. She sometimes calls him her "Best Husband So Far," but he's the best husband anybody ever had, ever.

Jill is a unique and supremely gifted writer; she is a female Mark Twain. The only thing better than her talent is her heart. She gives 10 percent of her money, 90 percent of her time, and 100 percent of her love to others.

But what would have become of her if she did not also possess a

Warrior's courage? Every artist encounters some rejection and must find some way to fight through it, but imagine the bravery it took for her to write her first book when her husband had betrayed her, stolen from her, abandoned her—and then the one professional she knew in publishing told her she couldn't write.

REMEMBER BOB'S TALE OF ABRAHIM? THE BANDIT WHO climbed over the wall in the middle of the night when he was a kid? I asked Bob what had become of such a mysterious and legendary man. Bob told me, with sadness, that Abrahim had died. I was imagining that such a larger-than-life man, whom even the Pashtuns thought of as the boogeyman, must have died in some epic fashion. But what actually killed Abrahim was an infection.

It seemed a rather undramatic way to go—until an infection almost killed me too.

It didn't occur to me at the time, but when it was nearly over, and I was, as we Tennesseans say, out of the woods, it struck me that Bob knew even better than I did how much danger I was in, and that knowledge shaped what he was feeling as he came to the hospital twice a day to be there for me.

NINE

WHERE THE FINGER POINTS

MUSIC IS POWERFUL FOR ME; IT IS CERTAINLY ONE OF THE languages of God. Music, created from the soul and for the soul, reaches deeper than conscious thought. I love to hear it and sometimes love to play it, mostly on guitar or piano and once in a while on the drums. When we're listening to music, it's as if our hearts are playing along with it.

Silence is a part of music. Without Silence there would be no music. Silence is not only the older sibling of music; it is a vital part of the music itself, creating punctuations and rhythms.

Sometimes when I sit in silence, I begin to write, and the words move through my fingers in a way I experience as musical. Sometimes I even write in verse and think of these rhyming lines as songs. When I'm writing a screenplay or a novel, I mostly use a keyboard because typing into computer files is so efficient.

But I love to hold a pen and write onto paper. One of my favorite experiences of writing is the stage of a story when I can hold its pages in my hands and make revisions directly onto the physical presence of a manuscript. (If you've never read *Care of the Soul* by Thomas Moore, you should. It's one of my favorite books, and it speaks to the way our souls love the physical word and can be nurtured in it.)

I nearly lost my ability to write this way and to play music. I came close to losing my physical life.

It happened this way.

❦

I LOVE EXERCISE, AND I ESPECIALLY LOVE IT WHEN IT'S HARD. I'm addicted to the feeling that I did something today that will make me stronger tomorrow. And since so much of my work involves stillness and solitude, it's a joy for me to get up and do something active. God has created us in human bodies. It's easy for me to believe that honoring those bodies is part of living the Braveheart Life.

A couple of years ago a friend invited me to visit a unique workout group led by Laird Hamilton. There are so many stories about Laird that he is accurately called a living legend. My favorite is this one—and yes, it's true.

Laird is known for surfing monster waves. He's also known as the pioneer and inventor of tow-in surfing, where a guy on a Jet Ski tows the surfer like a water skier to the perfect spot to catch a wave. One day while seeking out the ultimate monster wave, Laird had a friend of his tow him out in the ocean. The waves were so massive it was impossible to ride them any other way. Then a wave came in, and it was so big and fast it caught the Jet Ski and Laird with it. Laird, the Jet Ski, and the buddy all went tumbling under the ferociously massive wave. When they came up, the friend's femoral artery had been severed by the fin of the ski, and he was bleeding to death in the giant surf.

Laird stripped off his wet suit and used it as a tourniquet on his buddy's leg. Then he sprint-swam several hundred yards to the Jet Ski, which had been washed out to sea by the wave. When he reached it, the Jet Ski wouldn't start because its safety circuit had been triggered when its rider fell off. Laird found an iPod in the stow compartment, stripped the wire of its ear buds with his teeth, and used it to hot-wire

56

the Jet Ski. He rode it back to find his friend bobbing helplessly in the giant waves.

Laird wrestled the guy up onto the Jet Ski and drove him into shore. Guys who were there called the paramedics, and one of them loaned Laird an extra pair of shorts so he'd have something to wear. The paramedics arrived, and they flew the buddy out to the hospital.

The surf was still up, so Laird put his wetsuit back on and went out to catch some more waves.

Laird and his wife, Gabrielle Reece, lead, instruct, and inspire their workout group, and I feel enormously blessed that they, and the other extraordinary men and women who participate with them, have let me be a part of it. Fitness is a part of the Braveheart Life. Fitness doesn't mean turning yourself into Laird—we couldn't do that even if we wanted to—but it does mean honoring your physical body and the spirit that motivates it by striving to move in the direction of physical vibrancy.

It's wonderful to be a part of a group all working for the same purpose. It's challenging too. It's easy to get caught up in following others. In fact, that's the power of a group: you learn from them as well as from the leader, and you're driven to keep going. You become inspired and encouraged.

The process does involve pain, though.

Ignoring pain is part of the Braveheart Journey. So is admitting it.

I had been doing that for a full summer with Laird and the great group of guys he leads in workouts. I was feeling good and adventurous, too, so when one of the guys offered to help me learn to paddleboard, I took him up on it.

We went out on a beautiful day and had fun. During the hour or so we were out, I fell off the board and into a bed of kelp. I had to struggle a bit to get to the surface, swimming up through the tentacles of the kelp.

I don't know if that's what caused the problem, but shortly after that I found two spots on my hand, tucked between fingers. They were so tiny I thought they were splinters, but they were more painful than any splinters I'd ever had, small spots of swelling with dark spots in the center. I tried to get the splinters out but couldn't. I saw a doctor the next day, and he thought they were blisters, though he couldn't figure out how I could have caused them between my fingers.

That night the swelling and pain increased. The next day I saw an internist. He said with complete conviction that the sites were spider bites, specifically those of a nasty little beast called the brown recluse.

He gave me antibiotics and prednisone, a steroid.

Two days later the swelling seemed to have diminished a bit, but the infection was still there, so he prescribed doubling up on the steroid. Two days later the fingers were swollen twice their normal size, and the bright red swelling had spread down into my palm. My doctor sent me to the hospital.

I checked in. They put me on morphine for the pain. Late in the afternoon, after I'd been there for six hours or more, a doctor walked in and took a look at my hand. "That's no spider bite," he said. "I think it's a community contracted infection."

A hand surgeon was supposed to see me too—my family doctor had asked for one to come by. But he didn't show until the next day. When he did come rolling in and took his first glance at my hand, he seemed to grow angry. "That hand's in deep trouble!" he barked. "I'm going to operate on it!"

"Operate?" I said, trying to get my morphine-muddled mind around what was happening.

"It'll take more than one!" he said, seeming to grow angrier with each word. "Five or six operations over the next year! I'll operate on you at four this afternoon!"

Dull as I was, I was beginning to grasp that this was serious. "At four?" I said.

He nearly exploded. "I have other patients to see beside you, you know! I'm not operating just to give myself something to do!" He stormed out.

I was sure of only a couple of things: my hand needed attention. And if anybody was going to operate on it, it would not be him.

I called my friend Brad, who had been a rehab doctor before starting his own medical business, and told him what was going on. I said I needed advice. "I'll call you right back," he said.

A few minutes later he did call back. "The best hand surgeon in the world is at the Mayo Clinic in Phoenix," he told me. "I've just gotten off the phone with him, and he's waiting there to see you."

"You mean, in Phoenix?" I wasn't the most lucid or the most decisive. Fortunately my friend was.

"You need to go there, right now."

"To Phoenix? But . . . I mean . . . isn't there somebody in L.A. who could help me?"

"Randy," he said, "the decision you make in the next five minutes will affect every minute for the rest of your life."

I'd never been told anything like that. I've had quite a few injuries in my life. I've broken bones in sports and broken them in fights—once in karate sparring and once by punching a burglar. Those required hospital visits, but the only time I'd ever had to stay overnight was for replacing a knee. When I'd been sent into the hospital for the infection in my hand, I figured it was because the doctor wanted me to have antibiotics that I couldn't administer by myself. I had no concept that there was anything like real danger present.

But something flashed in my memory when my friend told me that I had to decide "right now."

When I was in college, to fulfill the language requirement, I signed up for Introductory Russian. It seemed dark and mysterious and an exotic challenge. I ended up studying the language and the literature all four undergraduate years, mainly because of two extraordinary teachers, a married couple named Hilda and Mikhail Pavlov. The Pavlovs were survivors of the siege of Leningrad during World War II, when a German army of 100,000 men surrounded that Russian city in a battle that would last nine hundred days, subjecting the citizens to the terrors of shelling and cold and starvation.

The Pavlovs were beautiful people who, between the two of them, spoke nearly twenty languages. What impressed me even more than their linguistic brilliance was their love of life. They looked into the eyes of every student, they listened, and they laughed too. I was amazed that people who had known so much suffering could live with such delight in the present without looking back. I once asked Mrs. Pavlov if she had been able to take anything with her when she and her husband left Russia. She paused for only the briefest moment and said, "Three times in my life someone has come running into a room where I was and shouted, 'If you don't run right now, you will die.' I couldn't take anything with me." She paused again, only slightly longer, and added, "I have no regrets."

Now someone had told me something similar: *Go, or you're in deep trouble.*

I called my sons and told them I had to get to Phoenix. Now. Whatever it took.

"Got it," Andrew said. A half hour later we were on our way out to the hospital, to the Burbank airport. My doctor buddy was coming too.

I had just enough time to call my writer friend Jill Conner Browne and tell her I was going. Since we talk on the phone every day, I didn't want her to worry.

We flew to Phoenix; someone from the hospital met us at the airport and drove us to Mayo. The doctor, Tony Smith, was true to his word and was still there, waiting for us. It was late afternoon, long after his workday should've been over, when we walked into his office. He looked at my hand and said, "I'll operate now."

The next few hours were a blur. I woke up in a recovery room with Andrew, Cullen, and Brad, my doctor friend, there. Bob would show up shortly after. "Your hand's in trouble," Dr. Smith said. "This is bad."

"Bad?" I said. I guess all I had were questions. I sure had no answers. "How bad?"

"You're going to be in the hospital for a while," the doctor said. "Probably three weeks."

To be in the hospital for three weeks was incomprehensible for me. So the idea that any of this could be worse than three weeks of inconvenience lurked at the outskirts of my awareness, and I wouldn't let it in. I felt sure I'd surprise the doctors with the speed of my recovery. I'd done that before in other medical procedures. When a doctor in Los Angeles had replaced my knee joint he told me he'd never had a patient bounce back so quickly. I'd do that again; I was sure.

But Andrew, Cullen, and my buddy Dr. Brad all decided to stay in Arizona. If I had been thinking straighter, I'd have been more frightened by that; then again, they were good at putting a casual face on the situation.

Bob from Afghanistan had moved to Phoenix a few years earlier. He showed up at the hospital and insisted they all stay with him; hospitality is part of Bob's nature and part of his culture. He not only entertained my sons and Dr. Brad the whole time they were in Phoenix, but he also came to visit me a couple of times every day.

Dr. Smith told me he'd operate on me every forty-eight hours until the infection was gone. His plan was to clean out all the dead tissue created by the infection and put me on antibiotics. Mayo had quickly determined that the infection in my hand was MRSA, a strain of staph that is resistant to most antibiotics.

Two days later he operated again. When I woke from that surgery, I saw grave faces. Dr. Smith had already talked with my sons and my doctor buddy, who now looked at Andrew and Cullen and said, "Let's give them some time," and they left me alone with my doctor.

"It isn't good," Dr. Smith said. "The infection is still spreading. We have to talk about options."

"Options?" I wondered back. I was still in my mode of asking questions.

"The infection has spread; we haven't been able to stop it."

"So what options are we talking about?"

I can't remember his exact words, but I remember his point. He might need to amputate.

And now the situation began to take solid form in my brain. They would cut off my fingers to save the hand. The hand to save the arm. The arm to save my life. He told me he would operate again the next morning; they couldn't wait forty-eight hours with the infection still spreading.

Wow!

My sons and friends came back into the room as the doctor left. Bob had arrived too. I was doing my best to face facts. I wanted to be realistic; I knew I had to be. But it was as if my thoughts had turned to shredded paper and the news was a high-speed fan. Before long, Bob and Brad left me to be with my sons.

I had been in the place of being the son looking at the Father whose circumstances have just revealed his mortality. I had a sense of what Andrew and Cullen were feeling. There was a look of grief and fear at the edges of their eyes, though both of them stared at me with an effort that could come only from love and courage.

I knew that what I showed next would be something they'd remember for the rest of their lives. It was time for me to be a man, and a Father. It was time for me to have a Braveheart.

I said, "Guys, I'm scared. But we'll be all right. I will be, and all of us will be. I don't want to lose my fingers, or hand or . . . whatever. But if I do, I'll learn to do without it."

This, I can say honestly, was whistling in the dark. I know because after they left, and I lay alone in that hospital room, the Fear settled in like a cat watching me with a predator's eyes from the foot of the bed.

I tried to pray and couldn't. My cell phone rang; it was Jill Conner Browne. "How are you, Hunny?" she asked. ("Hunny" is the way Jill says it and spells it whenever she writes.)

I told her the doctor's prognosis. And then I told her, "I can't pray.

I don't know what it is—whether it's the morphine or a lack of faith or what. I just can't pray."

Now, to many people who might read this, that might make no sense. If you think all prayer is nonsense, it must seem silly that I couldn't just plunge right ahead with the nonsense. And if you believe all prayer is a humble approach to God, it might seem odd that I could not consider my very desperation a state of prayer.

But Jill understood right away, and typically for her, she had a decisive response. "That doesn't matter at all," she said. "I'll stand in the gap for you."

That brought tears to my eyes then and brings tears to my eyes now, even as I sit in a favorite family restaurant, writing this story—yes, using all ten fingers.

Jill wrote a prayer, prayed it, and sent it to me. I read it and let that be my prayer.

Sometime that night I fell asleep. This may seem unremarkable for a man in a hospital room with all sorts of sedatives and antibiotics and fluids being constantly dripped into his veins. But a hospital is not a restful place; nurses enter throughout the night to squeeze a blood pressure cuff around your arm and stick you with shots.

Still, I found myself in some kind of slumber, though I can't call what happened then a dream. It was a *vision*, something I saw without participating in it. I mean that, unlike in a dream when I—my ego, according to dream theorists like Jung—am actively a character in what unfolds, in this I just *saw*.

What I saw was the Wallace family crest. Not the same one I'd first come across in writing *Braveheart*: a battle helmet with an arm rising from it, cocked to deliver a blow from a sword, and the words *Pro Libertate—For Freedom* inscribed below. The crest I saw was identical except for this: the hand in the vision was not holding a sword; it was lifting its index finger, pointing up.

I opened my eyes and found myself still there in the hospital room, with the monitors beeping softly and the lights dim, and no one else there but me. And I felt a clarity. It wasn't a certainty; I still had my doubts and fears. And yet they were smaller and quieter. I felt something; I might say I knew it: God was not going to take my arm, my hand, or my fingers. I would keep all of them. And I would use my hand, whenever I could, to point toward God.

THE NEXT MORNING DR. SMITH STRODE INTO MY ROOM SMILing. There was a certainty about him too. "Ready?" he said brightly.

"We're not giving up, right, Doc? We're not giving up."

"No, we're not. I have a plan."

They wheeled me away. Andrew and Cullen were there, and so was Brad.

Lying on a hospital bed as it is rolled through the corridors and elevators to an operating room is a strange journey. You go to a surgical prep room, where they check you again and again and again, and you wait and wait and wait, and you meet an anesthesiologist, and he tells you they're going to give you something to help you relax, and then you don't remember anything until . . .

You wake up again.

I woke. And I saw the faces of my sons. And they were grinning.

Dr. Smith came in. "Your hand was clean as a whistle. I didn't need to operate. The infection is gone."

Something I learned during that time was about the tenderness of men. A Braveheart is not a hard heart—it is the opposite of hard. Laird Hamilton, who, it could be argued, is the greatest athlete in the world, would readily say that a strong body is resilient because it is flexible, and real strength is fluid. Resilience comes from the ability to flow. The heart is like that too.

I don't know if I would have survived the ordeal in the hospital if my body had not been strengthened through a lifetime of training, and especially through the workouts that Laird and my friends led me through. But even if my body had kept going, what life would I have had without love, faith, and hope?

I would ask these questions again four months later when my Mama passed away.

ТО FACE A MOMENT LIKE THE DEATH OF YOUR MOTHER IS TO have your soul sifted as wheat. It feels impossible during this time to even think of moving forward when your whole heart is pulled backward.

So before we look forward in our talk around the Freedom fire, let me tell you more about how *Braveheart* was born.

PART II

THE ROAD TO
BRAVEHEART

TEN

ALPHA AND OMEGA

WHEN I WAS IN COLLEGE, I FELT THE THRILL AND THE THRALL of studying under the great Dr. Thomas A. Langford, who would later become Dean of the Duke Divinity School. His classes were an experience of surprise and inspiration, of challenge and Grace.

He freely quoted the supreme thinkers who cavorted through the massive library inside his mind. Whenever he told us what one of them had once said, it always seemed to me that he was sharing a thought that had seared its way into his own life.

One of those quotes was, "I spent my life seeking God, and discovered God was always seeking me."

Truth, especially the intense form of it that is so real it feels divine, is like that: when we find Truth, what we really discover is that it was there all along.

Braveheart was like that for me.

I am called the author of the story; the truth is, the Spirit that created it is the author of me.

It came upon me suddenly, and years later I would discover that it had always been there and had been searching for me all along.

Here is how it happened.

THE BRAVEHEARTS OF WOMEN

Before I can go any further in talking about the adventure of the Braveheart Life and how the story of *Braveheart* came about, let's stare into the flames a bit more while I tell you two Truths that might be surprising:

1. The Listener is as important in the creation of the story as the Speaker. It's fair to say that the audience creates a story—or shapes how it is told.
2. The first audience of *Braveheart* was a woman.

These are not casual facts. *Braveheart*, a story that focuses so fully on Fathers and sons and the Brotherhood of Warriors, would never have happened without my Mother. And *Braveheart* the movie would have never happened had it not been for another special woman. Her name is Rebecca Pollack Parker.

A few pages later I will tell you of the time when my Father's wounds and my own both began to bleed into each other, and his healing cast its Power onto mine.

This, though, was a time when I was out of a job, facing the collapse of my finances. I had gotten on my knees to pray that the only God in my life would be God. When I stood up, I began to write the story that led me to *Braveheart*. The name of that story was *Love and Honor*. I had spent four years working on it as a novel, letting the story drift and carry me wherever it wanted. When I finished, the manuscript was extremely long by the commercial standards of the book-publishing world. I'd written two previous novels that major New York publishers had brought out to nice reviews but to no commercial success; now none of them wanted *Love and Honor*. So I was financially, creatively, and emotionally exhausted when I first came across the story of William Wallace. But as I've already mentioned, I felt unready to tackle that tale. So I set sail to work in television until that ship began to sink, and I launched into the even more forbidding world of feature films.

Love and Honor is the story of a young cavalryman who goes to Russia during the time of the American Revolution. My love of America's struggle for independence, fascination for the dark mysteries of Russia, and questions about the collision of idealistic goals and grim realities drove my passions for this story.

I finished *Love and Honor* and went in search of a new agent. All the doors in television were closed to me, the book world thoroughly rejected the novel I had poured my heart into for four years, and I had never written a script that had been made into a feature film. So finding an agent who would stake his time and reputation on my prospects did not look promising.

I remembered a young man I'd met years earlier, when my television future had looked promising. His name was Dave Wirtschafter, and he had impressed me with his blunt honesty. There was no nonsense about him, and he exuded something rare, especially in the entertainment world: his judgment had integrity and was not tainted by the opinions of anyone else. There was something else about Dave that I did not yet know. He loved to read. That would seem to be a common trait among literary agents, but, in fact, many of them in Hollywood prefer the socializing and the selling more than the savoring of the work itself.

I asked Dave to read my new screenplay adaptation of *Love and Honor*, and he agreed to give it a look. I'll never forget coming home the next weekend to find a message from him on my answering machine. His excited voice said, "This is better than I ever could have imagined."

Dave then did something uncharacteristic for the movie business at that time. Instead of making dozens of copies and sending them out to everyone, he waited. Holding the script. Then he began to just mention it to people he trusted and respected. After two months of doing that, he finally sent the script to four companies, and three of them immediately tried to buy it. We had a bidding war.

Rebecca worked for a company that was short of cash; nevertheless, she convinced the company to make a strong bid for the script. But as the bidding price rose, she realized she couldn't make the top bid, so she contacted Dave and said something bold, which he related to me in a phone call.

He said, "Becky Pollack just called me to say that her company won't be able to outbid the competition, and that breaks her heart, but she wants to make another offer. She wants to buy your next two scripts, sight unseen."

Those next two scripts became *Braveheart* and *Man in the Iron Mask*.

Thanks to Dave, I had met Becky some weeks before in what we in the movie business call a general meeting, when young creative executives sit down for a few minutes with new writers. She was different from any of the other executives I'd ever met. She was brilliant and authentically creative. Most all vice presidents at movie studios are bright in an academic sense, but Becky was different. There was something open and humble about her approach that made her talent unforced.

She is the daughter of Sydney Pollack, who was, and remains, my all-time favorite director, but I knew her for quite a while before we ever spoke of that. I saw right away that her way of working was unique. Almost every other executive I'd encountered tended to work from fear; they'd scan a script and focus on everything their worries suggested might go wrong. Becky would focus on everything she loved about a story *and would stay with that*, trusting that highlighting those aspects would naturally correct any other shortcomings.

I can't say enough about how vital this is or how empowering an approach this is in every aspect of life.

We don't maximize life by focusing on what is bad and trying to dig it out. That is like poking into a fire and trying to extract everything that isn't burning. On some level of false logic this might seem reasonable. Don't laugh; this is exactly the sort of logic followed by most people who try to work in the creative end of the entertainment industry. But it, in fact, smothers the fire. To make a fire—or a life—flame brightest and hottest, we breathe all the oxygen we have into the places where it is already glowing.

That, I saw immediately, is what Rebecca Pollack did.

I must also add that it didn't hurt any that she was spectacularly beautiful and about to marry another of my great friends—she and I were positioned to enjoy a lasting Friendship.

So when she made the offer to invest in my future, I jumped at it. A week or so later I went to her office and sat down with her, just the two of us, to talk about what the first of those two new scripts might be about.

I don't remember my exact words, but I can still see us in that office, facing an unknown future and excited and energized by the faith we had just shown in each other. I said something like, "I have this other story . . . it's really . . . different. It happened a long time ago, and there was a real person involved in some history, but not much is known about him and . . . his name was William Wallace."

For about ten minutes I told her what I knew about him and why I wanted to explore that story. When I stopped, she said, "My God. Go write about that."

Encouraged by Becky's reverent interest, I sat down to tackle the story that I had held in my heart for so long. It's not that no one else had reached out to reinforce my passions and my hopes—Big Jim Cullen, my wife's father, who loved heroes as fully as anyone ever and to whom I'd told the first seeds of my story, had somehow found and given me a comic book on William Wallace that he had discovered in Scotland. But Becky did for me what she did for every writer and every script: she found the glowing embers and blew them into flames.

THERE IS ONE PARTICULAR PART OF *BRAVEHEART* PERTAINING to a woman that, I must say, completely ambushed me and moved me profoundly when it came.

From my first hearing of the legends surrounding William Wallace, I knew that when the time came to tell his story, my telling would end with his execution and with an echo, a hint of resurrection, with Robert the Bruce on the Bannockburn Battlefield.

As I have said from the beginning of this book, I don't make up stories; I don't think anyone does—not good stories, anyway. They are given to us; they unfold within a storyteller and within the spirits of those who hear them. As *Braveheart* unfolded for me, I ultimately found myself standing on the execution platform with William Wallace and his tormenters. I was in an upstairs office/bedroom, in a house in California, when it happened, but I was *there*, in London. I see it vividly, now.

I did not know when I reached that moment in the story that William Wallace would cry out, "Freeeeeedommmm!" I typed that cry, and sat and stared at it for a moment, as I did again just now.

And then I stopped, as it occurred to me that I would not want to see the actual severing of William Wallace's head. So what, I wondered, would we see? Then it occurred to me—in part the result of my previous experiences as a screenwriter—that it would be good to move inside William himself at this point in the story. When he had won, when he had refused to break from the pain and fear, when he had surrendered only to God and not to the king, what would he do?

I thought, he knows Hamish and Stephen will have come to be with him at this terrible time. So in his last moments, he will look for them.

So I put my fingers back onto the keyboard and typed: "And in the last moment of his life, William Wallace turns his eyes to find his friends, Hamish and Stephen . . ."

And I froze.

It was not until that Moment, that very moment of typing, that

I realized that he would see someone else too. My fingers found the keys to write: "And there, between them, is . . ." And suddenly, for the first time, I realized that his wife was there, smiling at him to show him that she had come back and where he was going, she already was.

I sat there alone in my office. And I wept.

ELEVEN

THE MOTHER

IN THE MINDS OF MANY PEOPLE, *BRAVEHEART* IS A STORY about men and for men.

But is it really?

A friend of mine recently told me that he used to think *Braveheart* was the most macho film ever made, but as he's matured he's begun to think that it's actually the most macho Chick Flick ever made.

The love of women—and the power of their love—are so deeply at the foundations of *Braveheart* that it may be easy to overlook their importance at first.

William Wallace's mother does not appear in the story; she has passed away before we meet the main characters. What the boy feels is the absence of a woman's touch in his life; he has only a father and a brother and male friends.

When he loses his father and brother, he is profoundly Alone.

I remember writing this part of the story. I was sitting at my computer keyboard in a quiet place in my home, just as I am right now. I had not planned the scene; the story had just led me to it. Contrary to the conventional wisdom taught in most every film school I know, I had no outline when I began writing *Braveheart*. I wrote that the boy is standing alone at the new, fresh graves of his father and brother, and the only family he knows are in that ground.

I remember thinking, *No one would want to approach him. Who would know what to say? And all the neighbors would know that to move to him would be to take possession of responsibility for raising a boy who is willful and would bring trouble, since he is the son of a father who was known to be rebellious.*

Then it struck me that the one who would ignore such fears—or not possess them at all—would be a child. And then it struck me that it would be a girl. William has a best friend, the burly boy named Hamish, but Hamish is standing with his own father and feeling all the grief and sadness warriors feel when they lose one of their own.

But the girl . . . ah, the girl. She looks back. She can feel young William's isolation. She alone finds it unbearable. She stops, looks up at her mother, and sees the sadness in her face. She picks a flower, runs back to the boy alone at the grave, looks into his eyes, and gives it to him.

And he remembers this for the rest of his life.

It took my breath away when that happened. My fingers were typing the words, but I had not seen them coming.

It was the same when I wrote of William Wallace's returning home, fully grown after his time away with Uncle Argyle.

I don't believe anyone has ever asked me why William Wallace comes home in *Braveheart*. His house is a ruin, his property neglected, and most everyone there has forgotten him. Why does he come home?

Because he has never forgotten *her.*

I did understand that when I wrote it. But once again, the story surprised me. William approaches Murron and finds the courage to ask her to go for a ride with him. They have a beautiful time together, spent mostly in silence. When he brings her back home, she wants something special to happen—a kiss, a conversation, something. But he can't bring himself to say or do anything like that.

I remember that exact Moment, too, sitting at the keyboard. I completely understood the awkwardness that both of them felt. I felt that something important needed to happen, but I had no idea what it was. Then I thought, *He'd give her something.* And as I often do when writing, I started with that thread and wrote, "He reaches out and takes her hand, and gives her . . ."

I didn't know what it was that he would give her. And then it came: *he gives her the flower that he has saved all those years.* He was telling her, in a way words could not convey, how much she means to him.

And she understands. Suddenly, fully, and beautifully, she understands.

That is who women are.

And who this one is drives his whole life. She is Love beyond abstractions and sentimental ideas. She is Love embodied, Love real and unconfined.

But the world has other ideas. And because William knows real Love, he cannot live with the rules that deny Love. For William, because of Murron, Love and Life are now the same thing. His father and brother and many of his neighbors have been killed fighting for a cause that William seems to understand but will not join. "I know who my father is," he says. "But if I can live in peace, I will."

But interfere with the Love he has found, separate him from it in any way, and he will come against you with the full force of his life.

TWELVE

CONNECTING

The Power of True Partnership

THE POWER OF BEING A LISTENER AND PARTICIPATING IN THE hearing and the creation of a Story all at the same time is neither passive nor less significant than being a Speaker.

Every performer knows the power of an audience. The singer, the comedian, the actor are all dependent on the people who face them with open ears and open hearts. The preacher is intimately bound to his congregation. When I was younger, I read this memorable thought from the twentieth-century Lebanese poet Kahlil Gibran: "It takes two of us to discover truth: one to utter it and one to understand it."[1] Now I see the reality of this goes even deeper than I first thought. I believe now that some of the greatest experiences of life happen only in the presence of a True Other, and this wondrous amplification of life is the work of what we Christians know as the Holy Spirit. It is the manifestation of Jesus' promise that he will be where two or more are gathered in his name.

When we fall in love, we are discovering and connecting with a Power that unites so utterly that there is no distinction between who the Speaker is and who the Listener is; in Love, both are both. Everyone who has been in this kind of love understands why this Power is called a spirit and why it is holy.

I say this as if I actually understood Love and the workings of God. Each time I think I've figured anything out, I quickly come upon an experience and a mystery that I can't explain. I suppose this is some of the divine creation and God's infinite capacity to grow and lead us to do the same.

Still, I try to find explanations, and here is my current one—about *current*. God's Love is like a generator, full of Power. It is always there, and in order for it to flow, we must complete the circuit. We do that by loving. As we love others, God's Love flows to us and through us.

If this idea works for you, good. If not, discard it. I'll probably be looking at it in a new way myself, come tomorrow.

⊗⊘⊛⊘⊗

LEST I LEAD ANYONE TO BELIEVE THE CREATIVE CURRENT between Speaker and Listener—like the one Becky and I enjoyed (and still enjoy whenever I can get her attention, since she is now a top photographer and designer, and the mother of two extraordinary young women and wife of a successful producer)—I must tell you a story that shows how much I, and the story of *Braveheart*, needed her directly.

I wrote a dozen drafts over six months of work before I handed the script to her with the label "First Draft." I love the freedom to write with the knowledge that I will revise, and I love the sense that creativity is not only a single inspiration but an ongoing process.

Remember when I said that the conventions of screenwriting had suggested to me that the story should not begin where it did, with William Wallace's childhood? In that case I dared enough to put that convention aside, but in one of my last passes through that First Draft before I gave it to Becky, I caved in to another one.

The script was long, much too long. I had learned over the years that the center of the story is the main character, and one of the accepted rules of screenwriting was "Always protect the star." So, faced with a draft that was twenty pages too long, I did something I told myself was disciplined and professional: *I cut Robert the Bruce out of the story!*

Can you imagine the story without him? I could—I did! I wrote him in it, then cut him out!

The draft I gave to Becky still had all the other elements of the story; it was not that the entire tale was gutted, but Robert the Bruce did not appear as a main character. All his scenes had been there, but I doubted their power and their value. I dropped them from the First Draft.

She read the script and called me to say, "I love it. I really do. It's a tremendous story." She went on to tell me so many things that had moved her about it. We talked for a good while; she seemed reluctant to make any suggestions. Finally she said, "You know . . . when you first told me the story, you talked about Robert the Bruce, and he struck me as a rich character. When you look at the story to make revisions, could you think about him again?"

WHATEVER THE MYSTERIES OF LOVE AND THE DIVINE WAYS that two people can come together and become one, there is something I feel sure of: for that combination to be healthy and happy, each person must face certain matters alone, or at least independently.

My writing of *Love and Honor*, the story that led me to Rebecca Pollack and on to *Braveheart*, began with a novel rather than a screenplay. I had written two novels previously, both of them published. One had begun as a screenplay and the other I had begun in novel form. For *Love and Honor* I decided to wander in the creative wilderness, and let the tale unfold in its own way, telling itself to me.

This process took four years. I worked on the story almost every day. I took time out to earn whatever other money I could, through writing articles or television scripts or other odd jobs, but it was a lean and often lonely time. I realized at one point during that process that in an entire year, I called other people, but no one telephoned for me.

And yet those wilderness years were rich and most certainly shaped me and prepared me for *Braveheart*.

I often felt despair lurking, like a beast waiting just outside the door. I was married by this time, and my new wife brought me all the support and encouragement it was possible for anyone to bring. But there is only so much that anyone can do for another person's troubled spirit.

I have said that I don't think of myself as doing research, but when I love a topic, I absorb everything I can about it. And because I have always been fascinated by Russia, and my story was set almost entirely there, I continued my college practice of reading about it, especially Russia's history. I came upon a Russian saying: "When a man is born, he will walk one of three roads—there are no others. On the path to the left, the wolves will eat him. On the path to the right, he will eat the wolves. On the path down the middle, he will eat himself."

I knew what it was to eat myself.

One day I went to the store and bought a big square of yellow poster board and a red marker. In giant letters I wrote:

EAT

THE

WOLVES

I nailed that sign on the wall in front of my keyboard so that each time I looked up, I saw it.

We can love each other, help each other, laugh, cry, grieve for, and rejoice with each other.

But each of us must eat our own wolves.

PART III

THE WAYS OF
THE WARRIOR

THIRTEEN

NEVER STOP LEARNING. AND NEVER STOP TEACHING

IN *BRAVEHEART* UNCLE ARGYLE, CLEARLY AN ACCOMPLISHED Warrior himself, became William Wallace's Teacher. He knew faith, languages, and poetry as well as the sciences and the arts of war. He could not know all of this unless he, too, had been, and continued to be, a student.

The Braveheart Life is full of paradoxes. One of them is this:

THE TEACHER TEACHES LESSONS–
BUT THEY ARE SELDOM THE ONES THE
TEACHER THINKS ARE BEING TAUGHT.

Because of this, there is another paradox:

ONE OF THE BEST WAYS TO
LEARN IS TO TEACH.

General Gregory "Hal" Moore, who earlier as a Lieutenant Colonel commanded the Air Cavalry in the largest single battle in the Vietnam War, insisted that all his men learn the job of his immediate superior in rank and teach his own job to the man directly below him. Hal understood that teaching could be a wonderful means of refining the Teacher's own knowledge as well as that of the student.

The Teacher must always be teaching himself.

BALANCE

As I sit here myself and ponder the Braveheart Life, it strikes me that I focus a great deal on intensifying emotions and thoughts and on amplifying the experience of living. And yet I realize that true living also requires the ability to relax, to let go. Sometimes, in some ways, it even requires a form of surrender.

Balance is a potent and beautiful state. In my experience we are forever moving in and out of balance, and this is a natural ebb and flow, much like breathing. Balance is as much an active application of trust as it is a state of being. In fact, I believe that in real life, balance is never static.

Balance is not a state in which opposite forces no longer exist. The perfectly upright ballerina has not banished the existence of gravity. She has found the place where all the forces working on her body are precisely in harmony.

It is the balanced boxer who is the dangerous opponent.

The warrior who relies on a single weapon is easy to defeat.

HEALING

A warrior attends to wounds—of others and his own.

My Father's great wound appeared in the form of a nervous breakdown. Everyone who knew Thurman Wallace, before or after this period of his life, would have found such a thing unthinkable. I have said that self-confidence was his great Sword, and he had used it to cut a swath from a fatherless boyhood and a lack of a college education to become a national company's sales manager of a district that spread over several states. But the company, once a family business, was sold to a corporation that decided to try to inflate short-term profits by firing all the older, higher-paid executives. My Father was thirty-eight. He had never been fired from anything. He had loved the company he worked for with the same devotion, the same longing to please, that he would've given his father if he could have seen him anyplace but in his imagination at the graveyard.

My Father broke. All along he had been bleeding inside his armor. When he peeled off his armor, blood and tears were everywhere.

Since it made no sense that a man so strong, so in control of himself and his situations in life, could suddenly be so helpless, I at first thought of it as a bad dream. Just as I would awaken from the night terrors of childhood to find all was calm and comfortable within the Wallace household, so, too, I thought my Father would stir from the depression that had him weeping uncontrollably, trembling, and shuffling around the house in his underwear.

I thought my Father weak.

This was a horrible experience for all of us. While it was terrifying to have all of life shifting, as if bottomless caverns were opening beneath my feet—and when I have dreamed of Hell, it is exactly that image that haunts me—I can only imagine what that experience must have been for my Mother.

And, of course, the one suffering most was Thurman.

That ordeal, so clearly tragic to all of us at the time, has proven to be a blessing beyond measure.

It would be comforting and sentimental and self-aggrandizing to say that we suddenly saw things in a new way, had a burst of inspiration and enlightenment, and from that spiritual insight we turned life around. It wasn't that way. It was grit.

My Father bought into a bankrupt business and began working sixteen-hour days. My Mother worked too. During that time my Grandmother broke her hip, and we were plunged into another challenge. My Mother prayed a lot in those days. And we went to church every time the doors opened.

Slowly, dawn came.

This was a time when my Mother's Warrior spirit rose in her. She refused to complain. She refused to say a single word that would've wounded my Father even further. She dug in and showed him, and all of us, that she would never stop loving and never stop trying.

Years later I would hear a minister—Dr. Ernest Fitzgerald, who was then the senior pastor of Centenary United Methodist Church of Winston-Salem, North Carolina—say, "We have good days and bad days, and we seldom know at the time which is which."

To paraphrase this wisdom: "We teach, and we learn, and we seldom know at the time which is which." My parents were teaching me and giving me skills that were absolutely essential to my survival, and at the time neither they nor I had any idea this was happening.

Every warrior can break. There is always a hill you cannot take, a weight you cannot lift. Knowing this is not just important—it is vital.

We can take more pain and find more inner strength than we can ever imagine, but the real Warrior knows there are limits. He or she must learn these limits and then teach himself or herself to respect them. We must all learn that we can be wounded—and that we've already been wounded.

The wound we know is a wound we can address. The most dangerous wound is the one we ignore, either through Pride or ignorance.

All of us are dying. Most of us don't know why. Knowing why can help us live.

I remember one day in particular during my Father's darkest period. He and my Mother had chosen to move; he had bought the bankrupt business and sold the only house I'd ever known. On moving day Thurman's emotions were at their lowest. I'd always seen my Father in starched white shirts, immaculate in every detail, smelling of Old

Spice. On this day he stood in the living room as the movers removed all our possessions, and he had been unable to bring himself to dress. He wore an undershirt, what we would come to call a wife-beater, and had thrown an overcoat over himself. He looked tragic. He was.

That day is burned into my soul. And a day would come when I would feel just as broken and desperate.

And the memory of my Father and Mother's experience would save me.

⸎

THAT DAY CAME ON ME LIKE A WOLF THAT HAD STALKED ME since my birth.

Ever since the dream of being a writer had arrived in my life, I'd had a longing. If you are a writer yourself, maybe you know this longing already; it may not be different from the longing of any dreamer. I wanted to see my dream become a reality. This is the case with every true dream; it beckons us toward it. (That stalking wolf and the dream are brothers. Maybe they are even the same wolf.)

But it comes with other dreams; my dream was not simply that I would become a writer, but that I would be comfortable in it—that it would provide me money and security.

Think about this for a moment: to be a writer, all I had to do was write. Whether I sold anything or not, whether anyone read anything I wrote or loved or hated it, I would still be a writer.

But that was not enough. I wanted recognition. And riches.

The first dream was pure. The other dreams attached to it were perversions. There is nothing wrong, of course, with a man wanting to feed his family. But the Pride part—that does not seem so divine.

I remember the first day I received a check for something I had written. I sat at the kitchen table and stared at it, with a strange thrill.

In that thrill was satisfaction—and the kind of craving that the future junkie must feel at his first hit of heroin. Perhaps he was a junkie already before his first hit.

When I got started in television, my income doubled every year for four years in a row. Even if the money started small, the doubling results in a lot of money. I was able to buy for my family many of the things that others had, things I had not been able to afford during my years of struggle: a beautiful home, reliable cars, and dinners in restaurants.

More than that, I felt the promise that such a surplus of money would continue.

I cannot say I felt fulfilled; I didn't. I was writing episodes of television and grinding out stories to feed a system that did not feed my soul or the souls of the audience.

Suddenly the system broke down. The Writer's Guild, my guild, went out on strike. I had a contract with the company I worked for, but the strike allowed them legally to suspend all payments I was to receive. The strike went on for nearly a year, and at the end of that time, my savings were gone. And then the company I worked for began to break apart and dissolve.

I saw disaster ahead of me—or what I thought was disaster. And I began to tighten up, to feel a bleakness. I became so overwrought that I couldn't write.

So I took the best steps I knew how to take. I left the crumbling company. This felt terrifying; the people there had been good to me and good for me. I'd learned so much there and had been in the presence of mentors and friends. I felt like a man who believes the ship he is on is sinking, and he tries to warn the others, but they won't believe him, so he jumps alone into the dark, cold waters and then drifts alone as the ship, bright with lights and still ringing with party laughter, sails away.

I felt as my Father had felt.

When I realized that, I had a new hope. I had seen my Father at the worst moments of his life. He had survived, and I had watched him do it.

It occurred to me that if someone during that time had told my Father that by experiencing the agonies he was going through, he would be giving his son the tools to survive—if someone had told him *that*, he would gladly have said, "Then give them to me."

Still, I did not want my sons to see me broken. This, too, was Pride.

I got on my knees. I knew what every man knows when he kneels to pray for help in a time when he needs help desperately. I was a hypocrite. I didn't mean to be, of course—none of us wants to be shallow and false, and all of us know we inherently are. By the time we get around to asking God for help and trying to seem sincere and worthy, we're quite certain of how sincere and worthy we are not.

I somehow felt a certainty in that moment that God knew exactly where I was and how I had come to that place. So I dispensed with the preambles. I remember the words I prayed, almost exactly: "Lord, here I am. I'm broken. I'm afraid. I think I'm going to lose everything we have."

At that point I found the awareness that material things were only things. But I also knew that I could lose a lot more than things; I had lost faith and hope. I thought about my Father and Mother and those terrible days when everything seemed lost.

"We may lose this house," I said, as much to myself as to God. "Maybe my sons won't grow up in a big place with four bedrooms and three bathrooms and a swimming pool. Maybe we'll have to go live in a house like I grew up in, with two bedrooms and one bathroom. But it didn't hurt me; it was a happy place."

Now, prayers that work, in my experience, are the ones that bring us to listen as well as to speak, and in this prayer I was hearing something. Still, I knew where my greatest fear lay.

"What really matters to me now, Lord, is what happens with my sons. And if it's best for them to grow up without plenty—if wealth is a danger to them instead of a privilege—then please, make that happen. Help me show them what a man does when he gets knocked down, the way my Father showed me—"

At that point I felt the stab of Truth. And Truth is strength. I felt a resolve, a certainty, growing in me. "The way my Father showed me. But if I go down, let me go down with my flag flying. Let me go down on this battlefield you have brought me to, fighting to be the person you want me to be. Let me go down with you, not them, as God. Amen."

I got up and went back to my desk.

I knew I might have only one more story to write before I did the other things that the love of my sons required: to find a more reliable way to feed and clothe and house them, show them that a man takes care of business. But if I had only one more story, I would write what gave me goose bumps, what thrilled my heart, and not what Hollywood told me it wanted to buy.

Braveheart came from that Moment.

FOURTEEN

LESSONS ARE SOMETIMES HARSH

I HAVE SAID THAT TEACHING IS OFTEN UNCONSCIOUS AND even the teacher is often unaware of what is being taught, the lessons many times indirect and unintended.

Of course, teaching is not always unconscious; sometimes it is direct and deliberate.

My Father taught with stories. He delighted in sharing not only tales from his personal history but also jokes that were clearly invented—usually picked up from his travels as a salesman. I would call these indirect, but they had a direct lesson in the way they made fun of pretension.

Sometimes they weren't even jokes, just observations. He once told me of a man he knew who was the clean-up guy at a warehouse; he had spent his work years moving cartons of candy and sweeping floors. When the man told my Father he was retiring, my Father asked, "So what are you going to do when you quit work?"

And the fellow replied, "I'm gonna sit on my front porch and tell everybody who walks by to kiss my butt."

Only the fellow didn't say "butt," and my Father didn't either. When in the presence of ladies, he was delicate with his language; with men he spoke like a man. And he howled in laughter every time he told that story. (For Thurman, the howling laughter often came *during* the telling of a story; he could barely get all the words out.) But when he finished the tale, he wasn't finished with the lesson. He'd look at me and add, "Now that's a heck of an ambition, isn't it?"

⋘⋙

MAMA HAD AN ENTIRELY DIFFERENT PERSONALITY FROM Daddy. I took her reserve not to be shyness exactly but a profound respect for the privacy and dignity of others and that of her own. She did not judge herself by the opinions of others. She lived by her own rules. Her lessons were as focused and pointed as the tip of a sword. And just as penetrating.

Once we had gone to the Mid-South Fair in Memphis. It was a wonderland of my boyhood, a place of thrill rides and fireworks and the delicious smells of popcorn and cotton candy and ice cream bars dipped in chocolate and rolled in crushed peanuts. I had ridden the roller coaster, and it was as exciting as it would be to ride in a fighter jet today. As soon as the ride was over, I began to beg to ride it again. My parents had spent the time and money to take my sister and me, and their rule was "Once Is Enough."

Through the rest of our time at the fair I pouted and pleaded. On our way out I began to pitch a fit. "I don't want to go home!" I said. "I want to ride the roller coaster again!"

My Mother leaned down, grabbed my arm, and pointed to a boy in a wheelchair. "You see that boy? He can't ride a thing, not *one thing*! Now you appreciate what you have!"

It is easy to see this story as harsh. I see it as harsh as I write it now. It *was* harsh. And it would be easy to say that my Mother was tired and fed up and was having a bad day.

But was it a bad day? She taught me a lesson that I would never forget. And I still ride roller coasters, and love it when I do. I also look at people in wheelchairs and feel a compassion that goes as deep as the crater Mama stabbed into my spirit that night. And whenever I have had a chance to do something for someone who could never ride a roller coaster, I have felt a joy greater than what I feel in riding one myself. It would be hard to look back and call that moment one of my Mother's bad days.

Just as her lessons could be pointed and penetrating, so was Mama's love. She could convey Love by simply watching. By smiling. With a few words. After my sister had gone away to college and while my Father was still traveling, my Mother and I would be alone together through the weeknights, and she would make dinner for just the two of us. I had begun to write songs, and sometimes after we ate, I would drift into the living room and sit down at the piano and wander around the keyboard, playing chords and listening for melodies. One night I heard her beginning to wash the dishes, and I got up and went in to help. "Let me do this," she said. "You go back to the piano. I love to hear you play."

Years later I was struggling. I had tried to become a songwriter and had found no success. My parents had come out to California to visit, and they had taken me and my future wife to dinner. We were sitting at one of those Japanese restaurants where the waiter chops and cooks the food at the table.

I mentioned, "I'm thinking about trying to write a screenplay."

Mama looked at me and said, "You'd be good at that."

That was all she said, and I felt I had been knighted by King Arthur with his Excalibur.

It occurs to me now that the lessons went deeper and in more directions than I knew (or could have known) as a child. My Mother's sharp words to me while I was whining that I had not ridden enough rides at the fair were also a defense of my Father. He wanted his children to have fun; it was in his spirit to enjoy every moment. But the overriding responsibility for him was to be frugal enough to be sure his family had the basics. A trip to the fair was a splurge. My lack of appreciation was hurting him, and my Mother knew it.

LESSONS ARE TAUGHT IN SINGLE MOMENTS AND LEARNED WHEN THE STUDENT IS READY TO FIND THEM

It was many years before I realized how smart my Mother was. For most of my life I wondered at my Mother's tendency to change subjects in a dinner-table conversation. She seemed the Queen of the Land of Non Sequiturs. Our family would be talking about a trip, and Mama would suddenly say, "I wonder how Aunt Nell is doing?" This always resulted in stories about Aunt Nell and her penchant for interrupting preachers during tent revivals, and it always made us laugh. It was years before I realized that Mama's interruptions came when she saw that whatever topic we were discussing would lead, in two or three more exchanges, to a fight. She was heading trouble off at the pass.

Still, with all this, I think example is the greatest teacher. What is better than being with a teacher who loves his subject? And what is worse than a teacher who does not?

Maybe the greatest gift a parent can give a child is an example of joy. This leads me back to Tennessee.

⋘⋙

ONE JUNE I TOOK MY SONS FOR A VISIT TO TENNESSEE. MY wife chose not to come. I had become aware that my marriage was falling apart.

I took my boys to the church that my Grandmother and Daddy Rufe, my Mother and Father, and Aunt Betty had founded in the living room of Grandmother's farmhouse. It was now a thriving country church with a new sanctuary; it even had a stained-glass window.

It was Father's Day. And I stood with my sons and sang hymns I'd once sung beside my Grandmother, and I was full of emotion. The preacher began his sermon, and as he did, a Tennessee thunderstorm rose outside. Heat lightning flashed yellow against the wind crashed like Confederate cannons. The lights flickered, but the never faltered.

"I want to give my son ten million dollars," he boomed. "It's just something I want to do. But I won't do it. You know why? 'Cause I don't have ten million dollars. You're here today because you want to give your children faith. But how will you give it to them if you don't have it yourself?"

It was the most powerful sermon I ever experienced.

FACING THE TRUTH IS THE FIRST STEP IN HEALING, TRANSFORMATION, AND FREEDOM

In the story of *Braveheart* wounds are crucial to the drama and inspiration experienced by the characters, as well as by the audience. The deaths of William's father, brother, and wife are one kind of wound. Robert the Bruce's betrayal is another. Both cause him great suffering, and both stir Transformation.

Daring to love and trust when such a sense of loss is possible—and perhaps even inevitable, sooner or later, in every life—requires courage of the heart. Trying to avoid such loss by seeking to avoid the risk of Love and Faith does not prevent the wounding of our souls. It's as if betrayal wounds us by hurting, but the cowardice that seeks to avoid all danger is a death by poison.

All of us are wounded. All of us must learn to heal.

The time for healing is a crucial time. It was in my Father's life and in mine.

My Father was not a complete warrior or full man when I was born. He became one. He was learning, and through that learning he was teaching me. He learned through struggle; he learned through experience. One of his favorite sayings was, "Business is when a man with money meets a man with experience: the man with experience gets the money, and the man with money gets the experience."

Still, he may have learned the most through his times of suffering, though I would make a distinction between the suffering itself and the learning that comes through the Revelations and Grace that emerge during that suffering.

William Wallace was not taught or improved by his torture, but through the whole experience he found Grace and Love.

Looking back at this part of the *Braveheart* story now, I would say that the beginning of this phase of his Transformation was in his realization that to find True Freedom—for himself and for his fellow Scots—he had to do more than fight on the battlefield. The confrontation with this Truth, and the acceptance of its reality, opened him to other possibilities, however frightening they were. The Truth will set us free.

His absolute acceptance of this Truth—the smaller truth of his immediate situation and the greater Truth that there was a reality greater than himself, that God had made him, and only by living out the fullness of all God had made him to be could he experience the fullness of God's Grace—exposed the truth in everyone else.

Sometimes these truths were ugly. The king was unforgiving; even when dying himself, he was incapable of mercy. His son was too jealous of strength and too weak himself to make any choice or take any risk to change a situation.

Robert the Bruce, though, found a Power in the horrible revelation of all his compromising and the justifying of his betrayals for the sake of promises of worldly power. He realized that to gain the whole world and lose his own soul were nothing. The power of this realization was working in him, all the way through to the moment on the battlefield when he cried out, "You have bled with Wallace! Now bleed with me!" I

ie Power continued to work through the life and ongoing rule of Robert the Bruce when he took the throne and became Scotland's most effective king.

That part of the story is particularly powerful for me. When I first heard of William Wallace, and the guard at Edinburgh Castle said Robert the Bruce may have been part of the conspiracy against William Wallace in order to clear the way for himself to become king, I was jolted by the idea that all this was as if Judas Iscariot and Simon Peter were the same individual. Certainly in the Gospels we see the transformations of Jesus' disciples—especially of Peter—who denied Jesus and betrayed him through their cowardice and then returned, transformed by his Resurrection, to tell his story, no matter what the consequences would be to themselves.

FIFTEEN

A Warrior Is Always Asking, "What Is a Warrior?"

A Warrior is more than a soldier. A soldier knows only to fight. A warrior knows when. When to charge, when to retreat, when to sidestep, duck, feint, when to hide.

In the story of *Braveheart*, William Wallace is reluctant to join the rebellion of the Scottish clansmen. He understands the cost. His own father and brother died fighting. War, at first, keeps him from the peaceful marriage he wants and then takes the woman he loves.

In the end he understands that his greatest duty as a Warrior is to create a lasting peace. But as a Warrior alone he cannot do this.

The Warrior uses his brain. He maneuvers. His head is his first weapon.

But deeper than head is heart—the home of his courage.

THE WARRIOR PLANS . . . AND IS FREE TO PLACE THOSE PLANS ASIDE

I believe that when we speak of planning, we have truly begun to talk about Faith.

Planning is a powerful weapon, but it is only one. Planning is preparation, and in a certain way the plans are never lost, even when they are abandoned and the adventure of the battle—the appearance of new opportunities and the vision of new possibilities—causes us to discard our old maps.

My college professor and mentor, Dr. Langford, used to tell us, "If you want to make God laugh, tell Him your plans." Mike Tyson once said of strategies in a prize fight, "Everybody's got a plan—until they get hit in the face."

I have learned in my journey to live a Braveheart Life that God's plans are better than mine.

THE WARRIOR GROWS AND EVOLVES

In *Braveheart* William Wallace has trained. In a sense he was born to first become a Warrior. He's a playful and spirited boy who throws rocks with skill (in a mock battle) and fights playfully with his best friend. When his father dies and Uncle Argyle appears, he begins to train in earnest.

The idea of a boy who encounters the reality of human cruelty, suffers by it, then goes on a journey to harden himself against suffering, and disciplines himself to stand up to forces that would enslave him is iconic in storytelling. It has been around for thousands of years. We know this aspect of myth so thoroughly that when William Wallace as a boy rides away with his uncle, we have a sense of the journey he is embarking on.

It delights us—or at least it did me, in writing it—when William returns as a man and begins to reveal to us, piece by piece, the skills he has learned.

The first person he actively seeks is the one who showed him tenderness and concern at the site of his father's grave—the girl grown into a woman, in much the same way as he has grown into a man. It is impossible to separate a Warrior from Love.

But his intention to reunite with her is interrupted by another person who has matured: his boyhood friend Hamish, who has now grown to be powerful, strong in both body and spirit. Hamish demands that William show him—and the whole clan—who he has become.

William accepts Hamish's challenge to toss rocks, and what he demonstrates is not that he has grown stronger than all other men—Hamish's raw strength is, in fact, greater than William's—but that he has grown in the cleverness and mental balance that being a true Warrior requires.

He next shows that he has ambitions in life beyond fighting; he declares himself determined to stay out of the troubles. We have no doubt that this desire is sincere. William has seen the costs of war. The troubles of his people not only have orphaned him; they now impede him from courting the woman he loves and prevent him from marrying her openly.

When William Wallace loses Murron—when her throat is cut and she dies at the hand of the sheriff of Lanark—it is brutal and wrenching. It is a shocking surprise for most of the audience because the conventions of modern movies so frequently avoid the idea of real loss.

THE WARRIOR SEES TO HIS WEAPONS

When Uncle Argyle allows the young William Wallace to lift the sword, he is taking the first physical step in introducing the boy to a sacred object. It is a tool—but it's more than that; for the Warrior, the weapon is his manhood.

It is said that before the Battle of Thermopylae the Persian king, Darius, sent a message to Leonidas, leader of the Spartans: "We want only your weapons." Leonidas replied, "Come take them."

A Warrior cares for his weapons as he cares for himself and for his brothers. His body is one of his weapons. So is his mind. So, too, is his spirit. The great Warriors have led their men through their spirit, just as Leonidas had inspired his men through such concise and even witty courage.

General McAuliffe, who led the 101st Airborne at Bastogne, replied to the Germans' surrender demand with a single word: "Nuts!" The German officer who received the reply told the general he did not understand. McAuliffe asked if the German spoke English. The German replied that he understood the word but not what it meant in this context. The American general said, "It means the same thing as 'Go to hell.' You understand that, don't you?" The German said he did.

When I was a boy in high school, I was required to slog through *Moby Dick*. I remember more of it now than I do of any of the other books that I read in those days. Something I recall most vividly is the author's description of the practical matters of whaling. When a whale was taken, the sailors used harpoons to keep sharks away from the carcass. As it was rendered and boiled down into oil, various tools became slick with blood, grease, and water. When the vast job was completed, every tool was thoroughly cleaned and put into its designated slot in the ship. The decks themselves were scrubbed and scraped with sand. The process could begin again a moment later; but each time, the tools, the weapons of their war, were cleaned and sharpened as the vital objects they were.

When I began to write full-time, I began to understand how much my health and spirit were tools.

During the casting process in *Braveheart*'s preproduction days, I had dinner with Mel Gibson. It was just the two of us, in London, and I was glad to spend time with him. During our dinner, we began to discuss the actors he was choosing to play the roles I'd written, so, of course, this was fascinating to me. There was one role that had been particularly hard to cast, and he told me he thought they'd found just the right person. Mel was excited about the actor because he felt he was just as tortured in real life as the character in the story.

That was a tender time for me. I had lived with these characters for years, and now I did not have the feeling of control that I'd once felt while the script was in my hands alone. I felt, in fact, as my Father had on my sister's wedding day, when we were standing in the back of the church and Thurman looked at me and said quietly, "Well, she's got another shoulder to cry on now."

Mel felt this in me, I think. He looked across the table and said, "Randy, writers write, actors act, and directors direct from their essence as human beings. This script is you—it has a huge heart. I'm going to cast people who are in their essence the people we want them to play."

I learned not just the direct lesson then but all of its implications. If artists reflect their essence, and if we can become better people—if we can enrich our spirits—then we can be better artists too.

SIXTEEN

THE WARRIOR AND LOVE

THE STORY OF *BRAVEHEART* DOES NOT EXIST WITHOUT THE love stories. In fact, I would say that *Braveheart* is not primarily a war story; it is a love story. And the Braveheart Life does not exist without Love.

Stories are definitions. A Warrior, a man, is constantly defining.

I once read that it is meaningless to say we believe in God unless we can define just what God we mean.

That is also true of Love. What do we mean by Love? One way of defining it is to show what a man would give for life itself.

Braveheart, and my journey to live the Braveheart Life, has brought me into relationship with people I can't imagine meeting in any other way. I could have bumped up against them in some way, but that isn't really meeting. I'm saying that when your heart is open, you meet other open hearts.

One Friend I met in such a way is a woman who was so affected by the film that she started hosting groups made up of other women who experienced powerful emotions through the film and wanted to process those feelings with others who'd had similar experiences.

She told me that after she saw the movie, she had a dominant feeling that formed specific words in her head: *I want to be loved that way.*

She found herself sitting with a circle of other women on the floor of the lobby of the theater, and they were all sharing the same sentiment.

The point is men want to love women that way. There is something so deep within men that I believe is part of our created nature, something that wants to find the woman we would give our whole hearts to—and our lives to.

We also have a nature that causes us to look at every attractive woman and be attracted to certain women. Knowing what to do about that attraction requires the wisdom of a Sage. And doing the right thing requires the courage of a Warrior.

It is not just a matter of ethics and convenience. It is a matter of Honor.

HONOR AND THE WARRIOR'S LIFE

Honor is the Warrior's central currency. Honor is not pride; it is not about rank and uniforms and medals. Honor has a great deal to do with perception. Honor is about how a man is perceived by others and how he perceives himself.

Men who have studied the dynamics of men in combat say that on a battlefield the central force that keeps men from doing the utterly natural thing—fleeing in any way possible from the massive, impersonal terrors about to be unleashed upon them—is the fear that the men around them will be let down, will see them as cowards, will be slaughtered because they were abandoned by such flight. And the soldier who feels such fear believes he could not live the rest of his life with the knowledge that he had fled in such a way.

There was a great deal of Honor involved on the day my Father's Grandpa Rhodes told him he could buy anything in town by saying that he was Jake Rhodes's grandson.

There was a different kind of honor at stake in an event in the life of another iconic man in my life—one I never met in the flesh, whose life

THE WAYS OF THE WARRIOR

and death have shaped me deeply. He was my Mother's father, yet it was my Father who told me the story.

My Mother's father was Rufus Page. He died nine months before I was born. That fact alone has caused me to wonder because I know my Mother was so shattered by his death that she could barely speak of him without weeping. This was true even decades after his death. She loved him with all her heart.

My Grandmother, Elizabeth Ringgold Page, whom everyone outside the family called Miz Lizzie, was the most kindhearted and nurturing person I ever knew. I was her first grandson, born so quickly after Rufe died. I was robust enough as a baby to have been dubbed Buster by the nurses at the hospital, but I quickly developed a problem: I often suffered so severely from asthma, I could barely breathe. Grandmother Page would hold me upright all night long and sing to me and tell me stories from her childhood or from the Bible. To me, they were one and the same.

As I grew older, I noticed that sometimes she would look at me in a different way, a way I'd seen her look at nobody else, and a way nobody else had ever looked at me. "What is it, Grandmother?" I asked her. "Why are you looking at me that way?"

"Oh, Honey," she said and smiled. "You remind me of Rufe."

I was a skinny kid, and the pictures of him showed a broad-shouldered man over six feet tall, much larger than my Father or any of my uncles. But even in the pictures I could see there was something in his eyes that looked like mine.

Of course, I became eager to learn anything I could about him; my Mother would grow quieter rather than more talkative when his name came up, so I asked my Father, and Thurman told me this story.

Granddaddy Rufe—for such was his moniker in the Southern tradition of names—had always earned a living through the hard physical labor required of men in Tennessee, a state ravaged by the Civil War and loss of men in the First World War and the Great Depression. Rufus

111

was a farmer, a carpenter, and a road builder. When the state had the money for building roads, he was a bulldozer operator, an elite job.

But when he married the young Miz Lizzie, he decided he wanted to build a stronger financial future. Her family had a tradition of operating a country store out of a room of the house; Rufe decided he'd build a store.

But he had no money, no materials to build it with. This did not stop him. He found the wreckage of a riverboat on the shores of the Tennessee River and salvaged that wood. Through his farming and bulldozer work, he had acquired some land along the side of the highway that led into town. It was there, a few hundred yards from the old house where he and Lizzie were raising their young family, that Rufus erected his store.

But to sell things, you have to have merchandise, and Rufus had no cash and no credit. It was the Great Depression; there was no credit to be had for anybody.

But there was one place in town, five miles away, where laborers were paid in cash. It was called the Ice Plant. In the days before Tennesseans had rural electrification, the only way for them to keep milk and other food cold was to have an icebox, an insulated square of wood and metal that could be loaded with a huge block of ice that would keep for well over a week.

They made these blocks of ice at the Ice Plant, and men with big iron tongs would grab the ice and sling it onto the backs of wagons that would haul them from farm to farm across the countryside. The blocks of ice weighed fifty to a hundred pounds each. It was savage work.

The only other men who were tough and desperate enough to do it were black. My Grandfather became the only white man on the crew.

His first day on the job, the Foreman came up to my Grandfather and told him, "Now listen. I just want you to know that I cuss to get everybody to work. So if I forget myself and I call you an S.O.B., don't pay me no mind. I don't mean nothin' by it; that's just the way I am."

And my Grandfather looked back at the man and said, "I understand. And I just want you to know that if you do forget yourself and call me an S.O.B., and I hit you in the face with a claw hammer, don't pay me no mind. I don't mean nothin' by it; that's just the way I am."

This story became one of those tales that tell us who we are. From it I understood who Granddaddy Rufe was and who I was meant to be. Since my Father told me the story, and told it with such delight, I know, too, that he meant its message to land in exactly that way.

Rufus was dealing with Honor. And there was far more than reputation at stake. All his ambitions were wrapped up in that job. His family's financial future, as far as he could tell, was dependent on his ability to bring home cash, and this was the only place where he could hope to find it.

He showed who he was.

And he showed me, his grandson, who would never look directly on his face or be held in his arms or hear the timbre of his voice but would feel his spirit in this story, who I was supposed to be.

SEVENTEEN

THE BRAVEHEART LIFE
EMBRACES MYSTERY

SO HERE IS A WILD THOUGHT: WHAT IF MY *NOT* KNOWING MY Grandfather in the flesh caused me to be hungrier to know him in the spirit? What if Who He Really Is has come to me in a more potent form because I was denied the more convenient way?

I don't know; it is something to ponder.

Something I do know for sure, though, is that there is great power in *not* knowing.

THE POWER OF NOT KNOWING

The young Ranger captain dropped off two pairs of combat boots at my office. "*Two* pairs?" I said. "I'm only going for twelve days."

"You're gonna need 'em," he said. And then he laughed.

In preparation for *We Were Soldiers*, I had inquired about the possibility of experiencing some army training. I didn't know what I didn't know, and that's always a signal of danger and opportunity.

IT'S IMPORTANT TO KNOW
WHAT YOU DON'T KNOW

I believed some military training might give me insights I could get no other way than through firsthand experience. I knew I would want the actors who were going to portray the soldiers to have an experience in training, and if I did it, they would do it too.

When I told General Moore, the coauthor of the book, about my plans, I could feel his excitement right through the telephone. "Drive on!" he barked. He didn't laugh like the Ranger captain had, but there was mirth and delight in his voice.

When the boots arrived, with the Ranger captain's advice that I should break them in, I sat down, alone in my office, and took off my loafers and slid the first pair onto my feet. It was then, as I laced them up, that I had the first of many unique experiences about soldiers.

There are many varieties of footwear in the world. But I had never worn combat boots, and I realized these were different in one profound respect: when you put these on, you were going to kill or be killed.

Two weeks later I was on a flight to Fort Benning, Georgia, where a group of young soldiers—and one fifty-year-old film director—were about to begin Hell Week.

As the plane descended to the airstrip at Columbus, the small Georgia town at the outskirts of Fort Benning, I had one of those how-did-I-get-here moments.

Twelve days later, after some of the most physically challenging, demanding, and thrilling days of my life, I found myself standing in front of a group of young men who had just completed the last ordeal of Ranger School. I had participated in some of each of the three phases of the experience, and the colonel who oversaw the swamp phase had decided to "coin me"—when persons in the military see what they consider a job well done, they present an enameled medallion the size of a silver dollar to the individual they wish to recognize.

I was soaring from the experience—sore but soaring. When the colonel handed me the coin, the assembled young Rangers applauded politely. The colonel told me that the men would appreciate it if I said a few words. I looked out across their lean, tough, and tender young faces and said, "I'm deeply honored. Thank you.

"Uh . . . when I came to Ranger School, I noticed that you Rangers have a term you all use: *Hoo-ah!* And being a writer, I'm fascinated by words, so I wanted to understand exactly what *hoo-ah* means. I noticed you say it in times when it seems to mean, 'I get it; I'll do it.' You say it in times when it seems to mean, 'Let's go get 'em!' I once even heard a group of Rangers say a prayer together and end with, 'In Jesus' name we pray, Hoo-ah!'

"But I really came to understand *hoo-ah* when I was in the Mountain Phase of Ranger School. I was up in North Georgia doing the rappelling in the mountains. I had torn a muscle in my ribs on the obstacle course during Hell Week, so I had trouble breathing. There was a bruise from my hip to the knee from someplace I don't remember."

The young Rangers were starting to smile at this point because they all understood such injuries. "And my boots had blood in 'em because my blisters were bursting from the hike up the mountain." They seemed to really love that part.

"And so I'm hanging off that single strand of rope, and I'm looking down at that sheer drop of a thousand feet right off the face of Mount Yonah, and I said to myself, *Who-ah . . . thought this *^%! was a good idea?*"

They laughed. And I'll tell you something: I would have marched off to battle with those young men. Anytime, anywhere. I loved them.

I learned something else then: a Warrior is not afraid to love.

THE WARRIOR LOVES LIFE

That's what makes him a Warrior-Poet. Poetry is not just words; it is action in exaltation. It is the willingness to fight and the bravery to play.

It is never too late to have a happy childhood.

We can be to ourselves the Parent we always wished our parents could be.

The Braveheart Life is a lifelong campaign, not a single conflict. No one wins every skirmish or battle; the small losses are steps in the greater Victory.

When I am writing or directing a film, I tell myself that I don't know what is enough until I know what is too much.

In Faith, we first learn that we are not God. When I was a student studying Religion, I encountered the writings of Martin Buber, who, in his book *I and Thou*, explores the fundamentals of love. He said that all relationships with God begin with the fear of God. I have always taken this to mean the sense of overwhelming awe and wonder that we feel when we stand before the universe and begin to grasp its vastness and what miniscule and insignificant-seeming specks we are in it.

Once I stood on a balcony with my son Cullen, who is the soul of the Warrior-Poet. We were looking out at the moon rising above the ocean. "I love this planet," he said.

The Old Testament gives us this magnificent exclamation: "What is man, that thou art mindful of him?"[1]

And Jesus took all this into divine territory when he said, "The very hairs of your head are all numbered. . . . Consider the ravens, for they neither sow nor reap . . . and God feeds them. Of how much more value are you than the birds?"[2]

I believe God meant for us to appreciate the world He has given us. To me, that means not only to view it in sacred reverence but to celebrate it in irreverent joy.

My youngest son is named Soren Eli. His mother breastfed him for two years, and he started speaking before he was one. He referred to breast-feeding as "um-ums." He, like his eldest brother, Andrew, adores the sound of a car engine starting. So when I bought a new car with a super exhaust system, I asked Eli if he wanted to sit in my lap and listen to it start. "Yes, Daddy!" he squealed, and crawled into my lap. I placed my foot on the brake and let him push the Start button. The engine barked to life! Eli looked at me and said, "Um-ums!"

Clearly he's a poet too.

EIGHTEEN

A WARRIOR BELIEVES

"All men break! All lose heart—"
"I don't want to lose heart! . . . I want to believe! As he does."[1]

WHAT DO ALL OF US WANT? TO BE LOVED, OF COURSE. BUT what does it mean to say that? It's the way we are loved that gives us the experience of being loved. And therein lies the whole issue.

This is true with everything in life that I know of.

And that brings me to Jesus, who shows us a way of living and loving that contradicts everything our fear and pain and cynicism tell us.

The story of Jesus, for me, is the one exception to the rule that Truth requires both a Speaker and a Listener. Jesus spoke Truth even when no one seemed able to hear what he was saying. Yet his story did land in human hearts, and it is told and retold because an audience responds to what feels true in them.

The story of Jesus connects to humanity because we are born with a sense of its Truth. Whether that sense causes us to fall to our knees before it or flee from it, trying to cover our ears, we recognize that Jesus tells us not just who he is but who we are.

Something that seems preposterous to people when viewed through the eyes of cynicism and fear is possible when viewed through openness. Coming to Faith is coming home.

All of us see the world through our own eyes, yet so many different people see God in Jesus.

LIVING THE BRAVEHEART LIFE

There was a rabbi once who said, "If we don't see God in others, they will never see God in us."

Jesus saw God's hand in all of us. He also saw our weaknesses. He looked at the men he had chosen—even the one Jesus had picked and trained to be the leader of his followers after he was gone—and told Peter he would deny Jesus and abandon him at his most awful hour.

He knew that all of us, even the very best of us, were flawed, broken, and corrupt.

And he loved us still. Enough to die for us. Enough to live again. For us.

WHY I CALL MYSELF A CHRISTIAN

I've mentioned that at college I had a fantastic professor named Thomas A. Langford. Dr. Langford was a teacher who actually thrilled me as I listened to him. I, and the other students lucky enough to be in his class, would come from his lectures excited, inspired, as if someone had stepped into the musty rooms of our minds and thrown open the windows to fresh air. When asked a question, he would consider it carefully, as if for the first time; he'd scrunch his face as all his spirit and energy compressed into some kind of celestial point, like a star about to explode. Then the explosion of light would come as his face cleared and his voice, high and tinged with laughter, would recite a perfect paragraph of luminous thought.

Dr. Langford amazed me one day in particular. There were two theologians who apparently represented the most impressive thoughts of the century. Both were Germans—Paul Tillich and Karl Barth. Each of them had written enough to fill a bookshelf with his collected works. One day Dr. Langford drew a simple diagram on the blackboard, and in that one sketch he summarized the massive lifetime writings of both men, titans of theology.

"Here is Tillich," he said, and drew a circle. "Tillich would call this the Circle of Being. Everything—everything that has being—is within the Circle of Being. To Tillich, all of it is God.

"Now," he went on, stepping a few feet farther along the chalkboard, "here is Barth." He placed the chalk at a point in the middle of the board, and from it he drew a vertical line. "God is here, at the top." He went back to the starting point and drew other lines in various directions, like spokes of a wheel. "You, me, everybody else are at the ends of the spokes. Jesus is the center point. We come to God through this center point."

If you asked Dr. Langford which perspective he preferred, he wouldn't tell you; I know because I did ask him. I was frustrated when he didn't answer. I wanted the quick solution. At first I thought he might not be sure, that he had only questions and not answers. Later—years later—I thought he just didn't want to short-circuit the journey each of us needs to walk in answering the deepest questions for ourselves.

The truth, though? I think he actually didn't know.

I saw him a few days before he died. His heart was failing. He knew he had only a short time to live. "I have no idea what is on the other side," he said. "And I'm not the least bit afraid."

I once asked him, "If we were standing outside the grave of Jesus from the time they put Jesus into the grave until Easter morning when they found the grave empty, what would we see?"

He did his pause. "Maybe not the same thing," he said.

This was not the end of his teaching me to believe; perhaps it actually marked the true beginning.

◈◈◈◈◈

"Every man dies; not every man really lives."[2]

To really live, we must be transformed.

William Wallace understands, ultimately, that continuing to fight on the battlefield, using all the weapons he has used successfully so far, will not be enough to win what he now sees his nation needs: a lasting peace.

His vision has changed, and with the changing of his vision comes a changing of his strategies. Now he must attempt what he has not been able to do before. In fact, it is something he seems to have failed utterly at doing: bringing the Scottish nobles into the same commitment for Freedom that the clans have been fighting for.

To even attempt this could be deadly. Wallace knows that the very men he trusts his life to are the ones who have betrayed him in the past.

And suddenly I understood Jesus in a new way.

In the New Testament story there is no *what if?* The Gospel writers tell us plainly that Jesus knew so certainly that his closest Friends would betray him that he couldn't abide their promises to the contrary. (I am convinced the Gospel of Mark is, in fact, Peter's account of his experiences with Jesus. Many scholars support this belief, and some of the most compelling evidence for this assumption is the way Peter's most painful failures are portrayed.) When Peter hears Jesus announce the ultimate execution that lies ahead of him, Peter protests to Jesus that this will never happen, and Jesus calls Peter Satan and tells him to get out of the way. When Jesus goes on to say that all his disciples will deny him, Peter declares, with obvious passion, "Even if everyone else betrays you, I never will!"[3] And Jesus tells him that before the rooster crows at the next dawn, Peter will have said three times that he doesn't know Jesus at all.[4]

Most moving of all for me is what Jesus then tells the man he has already designated as the leader once he is gone: "Satan has asked for you, that he may sift you as wheat. But I have prayed for you, that your faith should not fail; and when you have returned to Me, strengthen your brethren."[5]

There is a Power that transforms. I don't know that William Wallace knew that his death would galvanize the men who followed him. I feel quite certain that Jesus did know, knew that his life and death and their Power to fundamentally transform are an inseparable part of Life itself.

Warriors understand the willingness of their leader to die for them, to die in leading them, and that willingness transforms them into Warriors.

Lieutenant General Hal Moore, one of the greatest combat commanders ever to wear an American uniform, has said to me and many others, "In the smoke and noise of battle, surrounded by the screams of the wounded and the dying, a leader will either contaminate by his cowardice or inspire by his example." That same man stood on the parade ground at Fort Benning, Georgia, and told the members of the Seventh Cavalry that he would never abandon them. In *We Were Soldiers* we portrayed the essence of that message: "I can't promise you I will bring you all home alive. But this I swear before you and Almighty God: when we go into battle, I will be the first to set foot on the field, and I will be the last to step off, and I will leave no one behind. Dead or alive, we will all come home together. So help me God."

There is a power in saying that. There is a power in hearing it.

⊂⊃⊂⊃⊂⊃

THE POTENCY OF LOVE SPREADS THROUGH EVERY ASPECT OF the Braveheart Life. And nowhere is this Power more precious than in the relationship between a Father and a son.

What William Wallace learns throughout his life—what he becomes—is the Whole Story of *Braveheart*.

He knows a Father, the one who is biological and who begins the process of teaching him. After this Father dies, another Father appears in the form of Uncle Argyle. This Father teaches him, too, as does the Father of his friend Hamish. We can imagine that William Wallace encountered many men along the way who shaped him into the man he became.

The boy, in becoming a man, learns in many ways. The primary force in this learning is Love.

In the course of my life, I've had the opportunity to meet some stupendous people. Among them are Jack and Jackie Harbaugh. Jack coached an NCAA Division I-AA college football team to win a national championship. Jackie, his wife, is reputed to be the more competitive of the couple, though I have never seen her without a smile on her face. She has a voice that seems always on the verge of laughter. Their two sons have become coaches themselves. Both have coached in the National Football League and coached the opposing teams in Super Bowl XLVII. Jim recently took the top coaching position at his alma mater, the University of Michigan.

I once asked Jack how he, such a tremendously successful coach himself, dealt with being a father *and* an expert in the same profession his sons had chosen. The glow that always seems to surround him brightened when he answered, "You know, I once asked exactly that same question of John Elway's father!"

John Elway, a legendary quarterback, had gone to Stanford, where Jack Harbaugh had also coached.

"Elway's dad would come to practice and sit up in the stands and watch the team work out." This was long after his son had gone on to fame and fortune in the professional ranks.

"So I climbed up into the stands one day and asked him the question you just asked me. He looked at me and said, 'In your son's life he'll have many mentors, many coaches, many men to teach and motivate and correct him. He'll have only one father. All you have to do is love him.'"

This story has been one of the most insightful—and useful—I have heard in my own journey. I think of it often.

One of the interesting aspects of the story is its acknowledgment of the special privilege and responsibility of being the Dad, the First Man in a child's life.

That's why the message Jesus brought—a message that is unique and so profound it is called "The Good News"—speaks to us at such a deep level when he says, "Call God 'Abba.'"[6] *Abba*, in the language Jesus spoke, literally means "Daddy." To me this means Jesus is saying that we can understand God's Love for us in precisely that way. Jesus was born into a tradition that thought of God in terms of a great Father—many if not most religions have thought of the deity in parental terms of a great Father or Mother or both at once. In some of the sects of Judaism, which Jesus knew so well that his followers often called him "Rabbi," the name of God was considered to be so sacred it could not be written or even spoken. (Christians have sometimes followed this way of thinking; the use of *Xmas* for *Christmas* originated with monks who treated the name *Christ* with such reverence that they placed an X as a substitute for the written word.)

Jesus turns all this upside down and tells his followers that they can love God with the same familiarity and tenderness that a child can love a parent, one whom a child could address in perfect intimacy.

The Daddy name is not the only example. Jesus points out wild flowers and says, "Consider the lilies of the field . . . they neither toil nor spin; and yet I say to you that even Solomon in all his glory was not arrayed like one of these."[7]

I take all this to mean that Jesus taught that life is not a random accident; it is a gift, made intentionally, personally. And the lesson flows both ways: we can love God as a Daddy because God loves us that way.

NINETEEN

My Daddy's Gift

In our talk around the Freedom fire, we've looked at several aspects of the Braveheart Life: Parent, Warrior, and Teacher. All are able to see that Truth contains opposing forces and embraces paradox. I suspect that a real life requires us to do this and yet to go a step further—to understand the holiness in a single course of action, to embrace a choice and a value.

The Embrace—not a passive submission but an active acceptance—of the full range of the gift of Life is the full flowering of the Braveheart.

My own Father gave me this Embrace, even after he had taken his last breath.

During the filming of *We Were Soldiers*, my Father visited the set. We had done some of the filming at Fort Benning, Georgia, in the actual locations where so much of the real story had been lived out; then we had gone to central California and Fort Hunter Liggett, a training facility with terrain remarkably similar to the Central Highlands of Vietnam, where the US Seventh Cavalry and North Vietnamese regulars had fought the Battle of Ia Drang.

For the last three days of production, we had returned to Los Angeles and a giant soundstage on the Paramount Studios lot in order to complete the part of the movie that was set in the tunnels used by the North Vietnamese. It was the first and only time in my career when I was able to film a movie and sleep at home.

Only home was not what I was used to. My marriage had fallen apart. I was living in a rented house so I could be close to my sons. I thought they needed me close; I knew I needed to be close to them.

I also needed to be close to my Father, though at the time I told myself that I was just being a good son and doing something nice for Thurman, inviting him to come out and watch the last few days of filming. My sons were out of school for the summer, and they could be there with us.

He accepted the invitation with excitement. He had been retired for almost a decade, after a stroke had laid him low for a while and prompted him to sell his business. He spent his time volunteering at the hospital, encouraging other stroke patients to believe their recovery could be as full as his. But he still loved to travel, and, most of all, he loved to be with his son and grandsons.

Those three days of filming were among the happiest I have ever spent. Daddy was thrilled with every detail—the walk to the sound-stage between great hulks of buildings, the magnificently constructed tunnel set, the lights, cameras, and, yes, the action. And, as always for Thurman, the people. He just loved meeting people, and the stage was full of new folks to meet. He must have met a hundred people every day, and he remembered each one, and they surely never forgot him.

His health was beginning to fray, but on the set he never showed it. We had a director's chair for him, but he didn't want to use it. He stood all twelve hours of all three days, beaming at his new friends, at his grandsons . . . and at me.

At night he was almost too excited to sleep. I tucked the boys in and went into his room, a bedroom that was barren in the new rental house, except for a twin bed. I leaned down and hugged him, tucking him in as he had tucked me in so many times, and he opened his eyes and said, "Randy, I've already prayed to thank God for you."

A month later, after he had gone back to Virginia and I was in California, engrossed in the editing process for the movie, Daddy had a heart attack.

The doctors told him they could do a quadruple bypass, and Thurman accepted the surgery with the positive practicality characteristic of every decision regarding perseverance and courage. "Let's get it done," he said.

The surgery seemed to go perfectly. He came out, woke, and got up and took the first steps of his rehabilitation. Then something happened. While lying back in his hospital bed, he vomited, and the coordination of his breathing, probably compromised by his stroke so many years earlier, caused him to aspirate the vomit into his lungs.

He suddenly had pneumonia and went into a coma.

They put him on a respirator full-time, to keep him breathing. After several weeks of this my sister and I found ourselves on a phone call with his doctors to discuss "issues related to the End of Life."

But Thurman, as always, had looked out for his children. He had told us many times, and had even put it in writing with his attorney, that he did not wish to be kept alive by mechanical means.

I was on an airplane, trying to get to his bedside, when the pilot came onto the intercom and announced that there had been a terrorist event at the World Trade Center and that all air traffic in the continental United States had been ordered to land immediately. It was September 11, 2001. Thurman died before I and my rental car arrived in Lynchburg.

He died, but his life did not end.

After his funeral I returned to Los Angeles and went back to work on the movie. Thurman had taught me to love hard work and to know its power to soothe and heal.

My first day back we were recording sound effects for the battle sequences and the various extra sounds that go into a movie. One of the background sounds we needed was for the tunnel sequence, where Vietnamese soldiers are depicted on radios and in battle movements. For this we had brought in some of the same background actors who had portrayed these actions in the footage we had shot on the studio lot.

During a break, one of these actors—all of them refugees from Vietnam—moved up to me. Struggling with his English, he said earnestly, "Mister Randall, I'm so sorry about your father."

I could see how sincere he was and knew that for one of these men, all of them so respectful and gracious, to come up to me this way was unusual. I thanked him and tried to step away; I didn't want to get emotional again, not there, not then. But he pressed me. "I am really, really sorry."

"Thank you," I said. "Let's get back to work."

"No," he said, sharply. "You listen. On set, your father talk with me. I talk with your father."

I had to smile. So like Daddy to walk up to a stranger, one left out of the flow of things because he didn't speak the language easily, and engage him in conversation. But the Vietnamese guy wasn't finished with his story.

"Your father say to me, 'Where your father?' I say, 'My father die in Vietnam.' Your father say to me, 'Then I be your father.'"

If a story could be an epitaph, this would be my Father's.

But he did something else—the last moment I saw him alive on this earth—that means even more to me.

I can't tell you about it yet. When I do tell you, this book will be finished.

THE MANSIONS OF THE LORD

As we were finishing the final editing process on *We Were Soldiers*, my friend and editor, Bill Hoy, turned to me and said, "We need some kind of music for the ending, and I haven't been able to find the right thing. I think it needs to be a hymn, like a requiem."

We did some quick investigating and discovered that the US Navy has its own hymn, "Eternal Father, Strong to Save," adapted in a tradition that stretches back hundreds of years to the British Royal Navy. But the US Army had no hymn officially used in funerals for their fallen heroes.

So I turned to my friend and composer, Nick Glennie-Smith, who had written a brilliant score for the movie (and for all my movies), and asked him to adapt something from the melodies he'd been composing for *We Were Soldiers* that might feel right. I thought it should be something simple and prayerful.

I picked up a legal pad and jotted down these words:

> To fallen soldiers let us sing
> Where no rockets fly, no bullets wing
> Our broken brothers, let us bring
> To the Mansions of the Lord.

> No more bleeding, no more fight
> No prayers pleading through the night
> Just divine embrace, eternal light
> In the Mansions of the Lord.

> Where no mothers cry and no children weep
> We will stand and guard though the angels sleep
> All through the ages safely keep
> The Mansions of the Lord.[1]

PART IV

THE HOLES IN
OUR ARMOR

TWENTY

IN DEFENSE OF FEAR

I'VE HEARD IT SAID THAT THE OPPOSITE OF LOVE IS NOT HATE but fear—that fear is the origin of the vicious malevolence we call hate. I think I understand the notion that there is a powerful mechanism in fear that changes our perceptions and emotions.

Still, I'm not ready to surrender fear or place it strictly as a tool in the hands of the Enemy. To put this in theological terms, God is Love.[1] So what—or who, if we speak in the language of thousands of years of spiritual wisdom—is the enemy of God and of all Love?

A truly formidable enemy of Love would be able to use everything that is healthy—food, sex, ambition, any natural desire—and turn it into something unwholesome. C. S. Lewis has suggested that many of the sins addressed in the Ten Commandments are the result of natural appetites carried to an unnatural extreme. Still he cautioned that sins of the spirit are more dangerous than sins of the flesh. "That is why a cold, self-righteous prig who goes regularly to church may be far near to hell than a prostitute. But, of course, it is better to be neither."[2]

In the course of my own journey to try to live a Braveheart Life, I've come to appreciate more and more the truth of biblical wisdom "All things work together for good to those who love God.

come to see that Fear is a powerful tool—a weapon, if you will—in the shaping of a Braveheart Life.

How powerful a factor in manhood Fear is! Every young man grows up with some measure of Fear that his Father—or whoever fills that role for him—might somehow come to see him as less than a man. Women feel much the same, receiving the message delivered in so many ways that if they do not behave in a certain way, they will be shamed.

Fear is a profoundly powerful motivator. And God can turn it to the service of Love. Overcoming Fear brings us massive joy and transforms us.

Of course, sometimes Fear is so massive that we begin to fear that we will be afraid, just as Franklin D. Roosevelt reassured America at the height of the Great Depression that "the only thing we have to fear is fear itself." Panic—and who has not felt it at one time or another?—is a horrible experience, and I would describe it as a loop in which the fear of Fear creates even greater fear and grows out of control.

During the making of *We Were Soldiers* I had the massive privilege of getting to know men and women who had been involved with the Battle of Ia Drang in the Central Highlands of Vietnam. It was the largest single engagement of American and Vietnamese forces in the entire war in Southeast Asia. At one point during the start of the battle, a young and inexperienced lieutenant went racing off to try to take a Vietnamese scout prisoner and in so doing led his platoon into an ambush. Within seconds the lieutenant, his sergeant next in command, and the sergeant third in command were all killed. A young buck sergeant was left in command of the shoot-up and the terrified group of men who were cut off and surrounded for a full day and night. That young man's name was Ernie Savage.

Through endless hours of suffering and horror, Sergeant Savage kept his men together. They faced assault after assault by the enemy, sometimes in human wave attacks and sometimes in crawling attempts at infiltration. The fighting became hand-to-hand combat. At one point even the desperately wounded men that Savage's platoon had grouped together at the center of the tiny knoll, where they had formed a perimeter, were firing weapons if they had a hand that worked well enough to hold one.

When Lieutenant Colonel Hal Moore, Savage's overall commander, was able to spare the men to send out a rescue team, they walked right into the middle of the knoll, unable to spot the cut-off platoon. The men who had fought through the horrible night were so covered with dirt and debris and blood and filth from gunfire and shelling that they were indistinguishable from the ground.

But Ernie Savage had led every single man who had still been alive when he had taken command safely through that terrible ordeal.

During the making of the film, I asked Ernie Savage how he was able to function and keep making good decisions in the presence of such massive fear. I thought such fear would be debilitating. "Fear's your friend," he said sharply. "It gives you energy and sharpens your senses. Sometimes it's the only thing that keeps you alive."

There was a time in my life, in the year immediately after my divorce, when I would wake each morning and drop to my knees and pray for the faith and courage to get through the day. Then each night I would thank God that I had been able to put one foot in front of the other . . . and here I was again. It struck me that God had given me faith and courage each day. And how could I have had faith unless I'd had doubts to overcome? How could I have learned courage without fear?

But there is something I have learned about Fear:

FEAR IS A LIAR

A man I greatly admire is Rabbi Mordecai Finley. He is the son of two American communists: a mother who was born Jewish and a father born into an Irish Catholic family. Both his parents were atheists, and he became one of the most spiritual men I know. He understands the importance of Grace. He is the one who first articulated Fear in that way to me.

Fear does more than cloud our vision and our judgment; it shouts lies into our consciousness: "All is lost!" "Nothing can be done!" "You are weak and helpless!"

I experienced this directly during a moment involving *Braveheart* that I now find comical, though at the time it was anything but.

When the movie was finished, the producers arranged what we call a Friends and Family Screening several days before the premiere. A Hollywood premiere is strictly a promotional event meant to use glitz and glamour to generate excitement for the movie's release. But the Friends and Family Screening is often more relaxed and more fun. The one for *Braveheart* was packed with people. Hundreds and hundreds of people were jammed into the largest theater on the Paramount Studios lot.

For this screening I had been able to invite a number of buddies from my television days. They were writers whom I admired.

Now, the presence of these respected friends was not the only factor in what I experienced that day, but my emotions snagged on their attendance. As I sat there, watching the movie—the finished product, complete in every respect, exactly as it would be released to the world—unfurling on a giant screen in a beautiful theater, what I felt was not what I expected, or wanted.

All the confidence, joy, and excitement I had felt throughout all the other steps along the way now drained away altogether. I had watched the film many times already in various forms, and this, undoubtedly, was its most effective form—the colors balanced, the music and voices perfectly blended, the sound effects added and beautifully mixed. But I was in the grip of something that caused me to doubt the movie at its core. I was feeling fear.

What if all my assumptions and all the passions at the core of *Braveheart* were wrong? What if we had lost perspective? Sitting there in the theater, I surely had lost perspective. I began to squirm in my seat. The movie was too long, too raw, too emotional. I felt sure of it.

When the screening ended, there was applause. To me, it seemed polite, restrained, the sort of forced response a crowd makes when they feel obliged to pretend enthusiasm. As the audience moved toward the exits, I drifted along with them like a robot, my feet leaden, my hands numbed, my face stiff. Then I saw two of my writer buddies, strangers to each other, walking out of the men's room. I hurried up to them and rushed to say, "I know, I know, it's . . . it's just too long, and we should've cut out a whole bunch of stuff, and . . . and . . . it would've been better if we'd just . . ."

I ran out of things to say because I really didn't have specifics. There was nothing logical I could say because all I was expressing, at bottom, was my fear.

My friends frowned at me as if trying to make sense of an unknown language and said, "What are you talking about? We were both in the bathroom hiding because we didn't want everybody to see us crying. That's the greatest thing we ever saw."

Suddenly I felt differently. I walked across the street to a place where a group of my friends had gathered for an informal party to celebrate the movie, and when I entered the restaurant, they spontaneously began to chant, "Wal-lace! Wal-lace! Wal-lace!"

Fear had blinded me. Fear had shrouded my eyes from the Truth, so I could not, at that moment, feel what was deepest and truest in my life.

Just to think about that gives me a fear of Fear! But by reflecting on this, by facing this fact, my fear of Fear begins to transform into a respect of Fear, an appreciation of its power as well as its danger. Such a respect is not unlike what the Father, the Teacher, the Warrior, and the Sage all want a son or daughter to know about a tool, such as a saw, something that can cut and build. Or knowledge, which can enlighten or enslave. Or a weapon, which can intimidate or protect. Or even love,

...ich can break our hearts and yet open them to greater possibilities than we could ever have imagined.

Remember this: what Fear does, Love can also do. Fear can transform us falsely, making it difficult if not impossible for us to see the Truth, but Love works a different kind of Transformation. Love sees the flaws, the weaknesses, the failures in our humanity and recognizes the truth of their existence. But Love sees beyond to the greater Truth that we are creatures who can be transformed because we all live in the eternal Soul of God.

The words I have just used to try to express this truth of Love may not be the words you would use. But it is not a thought I am trying to express; it is a reality, an experience, and if you have had it, you know what I mean.

My Friend from Afghanistan tells me of a proverb they have there: "A man who has been bitten by a snake will jump at a stick." So what do we do if we are feeling fear and experiencing the blindness it causes?

I think of Fear as a dragon, a great mythical beast. To me, calling something mythical is not the same as calling it false. Something is a myth because there is an element of truth in it somewhere, and one task of the Braveheart Life is to sift the true from the false. The dragon is there for us to battle. It is our dragon; it comes for us and us alone. We must face it.

Once we have faced the dragon and have slain it, we experience something transformative, even heroic.

Here's the catch: the dragon always has a brother or a sister. As long as we live, there are dragons.

The greatest dragon is Death itself.

Once again this brings me to Jesus.

When Jesus said, "I have come that they may have life, and that they may have it more abundantly,"[4] he said something that resonates with me in every area of life. I take this to mean that Life is not built around rules that squeeze the joy and adventure from living or around hatreds that poison the soul or around fears that blind us to every real truth. I sometimes understand Jesus' assertion as pointing the way to a life that is amplified into a fuller, more vivid experience.

That is the meaning of "abundantly." But what about the meaning of "that they may have life"? I think he meant that we might have Life— real life, not Death. Life across the board, life across time. Jesus came to slay Death itself.

There is no Braveheart Life without confronting that fact.

TWENTY-ONE

THE FEARS OF WOMEN

WHENEVER I REFLECT ON WOMEN, I FEEL A CERTAIN SENSE OF mystery about them, a sense I think must surely be common to all men. To men, who tend from an early age to push out into life and go bumping into life—at least this has been a common trait for me and my sons—there seems to be an internal quality about women, a tendency to observe, absorb, reflect, and process that is more dominant for them than for males.

But just as it is a mistake to believe that women are not assertive, it is equally an error to believe that men are not reflective. *Braveheart*, I believe, demonstrates both these aspects of men and women. The two women that William Wallace loves in the story fight back against brutality and oppression just as bravely as any man could, and William absorbs their love and gives his own as fully as any woman might.

I'm fully convinced that men who love *Braveheart* are moved as much by the tenderness and truth in the way William Wallace loves as they are by the courage with which he fights. Men crave powerful love.

So do women. And as with every quest in life, the journey to love involves the facing of Fear.

Fear manifests in so many ways and can be profoundly destructive. But if we believe the Bible's wisdom that "all things work together for good to those who love God"[1]—and I do—then it is powerful to ask ourselves what we can learn from the presence of Fear and how we can face it.

Fear causes us to look to our weapons and to ask ourselves if we are lifting the right one.

Women and men all sense that to draw a potential partner, they must first get that person's attention. We know the conventional assumptions about how this is done: the male of the species makes loud displays of physical prowess while the female is demure and pretends to ignore the display while fully encouraging it. As people get older, we boil the equation down to a more crass assertion: men want sex; women want money.

If a woman believes that all she has to offer is her beauty for a man's ego, or her sex appeal for his lusts, then she has insulted him as well as herself.

Of course, men are attracted to beauty; everyone is. But what is beauty, really?

And, of course, human beings have a drive toward sex and reproduction; it is not evil—God put it in us. (As I was typing this, my finger struck a wrong key, and I first wrote, "'Bod' put it there." A fascinating typo!) We have bodies. Our bodies give us appetites. We often think of bodies and souls as separate entities, but there is a profound—a divinely created—connection between them.

Jill Conner Browne has often reminded me, "People grow more or less attractive as you get to know them." I find this to be true and believe it's because a deeper experience with the soul of another alters what we notice and value in their physical nature.

We all strive to be attractive. The strange irony in this is that sometimes it is quite attractive not to worry about being attractive. I have always found women who are free of fretting about their looks to be far more interesting than the ones who seem to fear that if every hair is not in place, their world will explode. *Braveheart*, of course, bears this out; Murron is a girl of the Scottish highlands, free in her laughter and in her dress.

Once, during the filming of *Heaven Is for Real*, my great friend and cinematographer, Dean Semler, stepped up to Kelly Reilly, the stunning actress who was especially moving in her portrayal of Sonja Burpo. She had just finished a scene in which her hair was tousled and her clothing anything but glamorous. Yet everyone on the set was feeling powerfully connected to the heart and the deep beauty she was portraying. Dean, a master Director of Photography because of his technical knowledge but the *best* one because of his poet's soul, put it in words for all of us when he recited a classic verse to Kelly:

> *Give me a look, give me a face*
> *That makes simplicity a grace;*
> *Robes loosely flowing, hair as free,*
> *Such sweet neglect more taketh me*
> *Than all the adulteries of art;*
> *They strike mine eyes, but not my heart.*[2]

Those words, Dean told us, were written by English poet Ben Jonson, and when I looked him up, I discovered Jonson lived more than four hundred years ago.

Ben Jonson and Jill Conner Browne were observing something quite similar.

I think it's important to remember that neither one of them is saying that a woman, or a man for that matter, should not care about appearance. Ben Jonson, in asking for a look, and a face, "that makes simplicity a grace," is pointing to an active choice, a brave choice made toward Freedom.

Do any of us doubt that if we were to sit together around a fire, Ben and Jill would be the greatest of companions?

Not every woman is Jill Conner Browne, and not every man is Ben Jonson, but the experiences they describe resonate with each of us.

And all of us know fear too.

Fear is a liar. And I believe I know its greatest lie.

TWENTY-TWO

FEAR'S GREATEST LIE

THE GREATEST LIE OF FEAR IS THIS: *I AM NOT.*

The Bible tells us that God declared to Moses His name: I AM. "Tell them, 'I AM has sent me to you.'"[1]

It is fascinating to me that so much of what Fear tells us begins with "I am not . . ." I am not strong enough, smart enough, beautiful enough, good enough. Whatever we think we need, Fear tells us we are lacking.

To accept these lies is to deny who I AM made us to be.

I don't want to quibble over the name of God. I know that God is greater than any name, and I find beauty and truth in the ancient Hebrew concept that God's name is synonymous with life itself, with the breath of life, and that his name was, in fact, unpronounceable.

Some people don't want to think of God as a *who* but rather as a *what*. Jesus, and the whole Judeo tradition in which he was born, declares that this is best understood as a personal entity and that it has a purpose, an intention. And that this purpose and intention are one and the same: Love.

So perhaps it is truer to say that the greatest of all lies that Fear tells us is "I AM is not." Fear wants us to deny that life has a purpose, that we were created for that purpose, and that the life we have—the one we did not create, the one we were born into—is not really life at all but is some temporary illusion in an eternity of nothing.

When angels appear to people in the Bible, the first thing they do is stab the fear of the humans they are visiting. "Fear not," the angel will say. "Be not afraid."[2] Of course, one of the clear implications of this is that it must be terrifying to be visited by an angel. This suggests to me that angels aren't the wishful figments of our imaginations that would appear to serve our every desire; if they were, their appearance would not frighten us at first. I've never knowingly seen an angel. But I do love the biblical reminder, "Some have entertained angels unawares."[3]

Before we leave the subject of Fear, I want to describe one of the most common tricks it applies in the lives of women and their relationship with men.

It's called . . .

THE TALK

There is something that is so commonly practiced by women in their attempts to relate with men that it goes by a term most every modern woman recognizes; it is called The Talk.

The Talk is destructive, and it arises from Fear.

I would say that The Talk is not really a part of a relationship; instead, it is a weapon Fear uses to kill all potential of a relationship.

The Talk is simple. It goes: "We need to talk about where this relationship is going."

The answer is: the relationship is going nowhere. It is over the moment that sentence begins or probably before the words are uttered. It is over when the woman gives in to Fear and decides she absolutely *must* speak those words.

It is over because the woman is telling the man—and more destructively, she is telling herself—that her fears are greater than anything else influencing the relationship. She is saying that whatever faith, hope, and love are growing between two people will not flourish unless she takes control of it.

Of course, she is trying to banish Fear, not surrender to it. But Fear tends to go away on its own once it discovers we are willing to accept its presence.

What if we could invite Fear to stay? What if we could look Fear in the face and say, "I am aware you are here. I will be alert and as prepared as I can be to whatever dangers I may face. And I will not let you take over what I AM, what God, wants me to be."

If we can do this—as the angels tell us—we will "Be Not Afraid."

TWENTY-THREE

LOSING OUR IDENTITY

HOW DO WE JUDGE WHO WE TRULY ARE?

I can tell you, honestly, I *wish* I could honestly say that William Wallace is the character in *Braveheart* that I most recognize as me. The truth is, I feel less like the hero, who always knows who to fight and how to fight them, and feel more like Robert the Bruce, who wonders and struggles his way toward a Braveheart Life.

What do we base our self-judgments on? How we look? How many people approve of us? Whether we seem to be winning or losing?

If we took a snapshot of Golgotha on the day Jesus was crucified and asked someone unfamiliar with the story who the winner was in the picture, he or she would be unlikely to say, "I think it's the man on the cross in the middle." And yet the Christian faith tells us exactly that.

William Wallace's moment of greatest victory was in the death of his physical body. This bears remembering, if we seek to live a Braveheart Life.

I believe encountering the Spirit of God—what I am calling the Braveheart Spirit—changes our Identity.

Now, it is a fair question to ask, "Does God change who we actually are or change the way we see ourselves?"

The obvious answer is *both*.

I was thinking about this question when I wrote a song that became the closing theme of the movie *Secretariat*.

It's Who You Are

It's not the prize
It's not the game
It's not the score
It's not the fame
When every road looks way too far
It's not what you have, it's who you are

It's not how fast
It's not how far
It's not who cheers
It's who you are
In darkest night you make your sun
You choose your race, and then you run

It's never the glory, it's never the score
It's not about seeing who's less and who's more
'Cause when you have found just how fast and how far
It's never how much you have, it's who you are.

When you have found just how fast you can run
When you have found your place in the sun
It's not just you that you'll find
Has made the run and the climb
It's everyone

Learning to bend and not to break
Living to give more than you take
Dying to live, living to try
Feet on the ground, dreams in the sky
It's never how much *you have*.[1]

I love writing songs, but I find it's something I can't *try* to do. They come to me at certain moments, when my heart feels as if it's expanding. I don't seem to be able to compel this.

As I'm sitting here now, it strikes me that what we Christians call the Holy Spirit has many weapons against Fear, and one of the greatest is music. During the making of *Braveheart*, one of the Highlanders of the Clan Wallace shared with me a quote from a Warrior-Poet who had said, "The Scots love bagpipes; on the battlefield they are the only thing you can hear above the sound of courage."

Drums, trumpets, bagpipes, the human voice . . . the music of them can lift our hearts.

MUSIC—A WEAPON AGAINST FEAR

When I came to California, I was writing songs. They weren't particularly good songs—at least no one else seemed to like them much, and I'm not sure I did either. I loved writing, the experience of opening up, getting out of my own way, finding (or being found by) a melody that unites with words and becomes something lyrical and new. I struggled a great deal during this time. My life was haunted by depression, loneliness, and poverty.

The journey was shaping me. There were many times I thought it was breaking me.

Back at Duke, Dr. Langford, my beloved mentor, who had begun to recognize that my calling was more to writing than to the ordained ministry, had once told me that sometimes a writer must leave home to begin to write about home.

For me, that has taken a different form. *Braveheart*, in a real sense, was me writing about home—about the deeper and more distant home that lay at my roots. And there was something about the form the story took, about the way the Spirit had shaped me, and that was in something I have to grope around to describe.

When people in the film business saw *Braveheart*, some of them began to ask, "Why does Randall Wallace write that way?"

There were two big answers, both of them connected to the Baptist churches I spent so much time in as a boy: the King James Bible and classic hymns.

The King James is by far my favorite translation of the Bible. There is grandeur in its language. Those who translated it understood that fully communicating the Spirit of the Scriptures required an appreciation of the poetry in the prose. "Silver and gold have I none; but such as I have give I thee,"[2] could be phrased in other ways, but it would not capture the heart in the same way. "Consider the lilies of the field, how they grow; they toil not, neither do they spin . . . even Solomon in all his glory was not arrayed like one of these."[3]

The soul responds to music and poetry and art. Here's something else that came to me in the form of rhyme and melody.

When the Midnight Turns to Rose

We were made among the stars
Born of fire and thunder
Fashioned from divine desires
Carrying God's hunger.

We had our birth on planet earth
Where moth and rust corrode
All the lies that plague our eyes
Someday will explode

When the darkness goes
When the midnight turns to rose

To make the choice from death to life
Is just a slight correction
We don't choose our starting point
Only our direction

Tears are but a passing pain
There to shade the story
We are only going home
When we aim for Glory.

When the darkness goes
When the midnight turns to rose.[4]

As I look at this and stare into the flames, is it any wonder that the Spirit is so often portrayed visually as a fire? I realize that in writing songs, and pretty much everything else I've ever written—whether novels, screenplays, or letters to people I love—what I'm really seeking is to feel again that Spirit, that divine connection, that Holy Power I felt when I stood with my family and neighbors and we all felt our hearts lifted in the same direction when we gave our full voices to hymns.

The hymns we sang in church stirred the soul—and the mind and heart too. They had lyrics like these:

I am resolved no longer to linger
Charmed by the world's delight,
Things that are higher, things that are nobler,
These have allured my sight.[5]

Call us rednecks and hillbillies if you wish—but we sang words written by some of the greatest poets in history, set to music composed by the likes of Beethoven, Bach, and Handel.

Joyful, joyful, we adore Thee,
God of glory, Lord of love;
Hearts unfold like flowers before Thee,
Op'ning to the sun above.
Melt the clouds of sin and sadness;
Drive the dark of doubt away;
Giver of immortal gladness,
Fill us with the light of day!

All Thy works with joy surround Thee,
Earth and heav'n reflect Thy rays,
Stars and angels sing around Thee,
Center of unbroken praise.
Field and forest, vale and mountain,
Flow'ry meadow, flashing sea,
Singing bird and flowing fountain
Call us to rejoice in Thee.

Thou art giving and forgiving,
Ever blessing, ever blest,
Wellspring of the joy of living,
Ocean depth of happy rest!
Thou our Father, Christ our Brother—
All who live in love are Thine;
Teach us how to love each other,
Lift us to the joy divine.

Mortals, join the happy chorus,
Which the morning stars began;
Father love is reigning o'er us,
Brother love binds man to man.
Ever singing, march we onward,

Victors in the midst of strife;
Joyful music leads us Sunward
In the triumph song of life.[6]

Now, you either see the power and passion in these words—you hear the music from Beethoven's "Ode to Joy"—or you don't. But don't judge the song—or yourself—until you have sung it in a church somewhere, surrounded with people just like you, people who may wish their voices were better and their lives were better, but such as they have, they are giving . . . to God and to each other.

You will find yourself transformed.

Just remember: there is no holding back.

SO WHAT DOES IT MEAN TO GIVE YOUR ALL?

The struggle between the rules of a Religion and the life of Faith—having the words of life written not on your skin but in your heart—is one of the great battles of the Braveheart Life.

William Wallace was Scotland's greatest hero. To Edward I of England, known as Longshanks, he was an outlaw, and Longshanks had William Wallace's body ripped apart; but he could not kill his spirit.

To the Romans who ruled the world's civil authority, and the religious leaders who thought of themselves as keepers of supreme religious authority, Jesus was an outlaw, and he was crucified as a common criminal between two thieves.

In *Braveheart*, I imagined that Scots, and Robert the Bruce in particular, were themselves shaped by William Wallace's sacrifice. They understood that outside authorities were not the arbiters of what True Life was for them, and that to find that Life, they had to become as committed to Freedom as William Wallace was.

Jesus lived and taught and demonstrated a Life beyond the limits of civil and religious authorities. That is not to say Jesus lived without; his prayer in the Garden of Gethsemane, "Father . . . remove this cup from me: nevertheless not my will, but thine, be done,"[7] is proof that he was committed to do what he knew God wanted, even if it cost him the human life he clearly treasured.

William Wallace was inspired by Jesus—at least the one I wrote about was, and there is clear evidence that the historical William Wallace was too. He fought alongside a personal chaplain; during his exile after the Scottish defeat at Falkirk, he was reported to have traveled to France and to Rome to seek help for his cause and personally petitioned the Vatican for assistance for Scotland.

William Wallace was a follower of Christ, and both he and the Jesus he put his faith in were considered by their enemies to live outside the law.

I believe we must consider what this means.

PART V

OUTLAW CHRISTIANITY

TWENTY-FOUR

HUCK FINN

The Great Outlaw

WHEN I WAS A BOY IN SCHOOL, DREAMING OF SOMEDAY becoming a writer, my teachers would speak of the nonexistence of the "Great American Novel" and the academic dream that would someday be created. When I was about fifteen, I discovered my teachers were wrong. The Great American Novel had already been written: it's called *Adventures of Huckleberry Finn.*

Mark Twain was not without his flaws, and neither was his novel, but it is filled with brilliant humor and insight into the savageries and heroics of humanity. Midway through its brief length is a single scene that deserves its championship among novels.

Through all of the story, the boy Huckleberry Finn, son of a drunken derelict of a father, has been seeking to escape life in the small Missouri town where he was born. Huck is fleeing not just his father's brutality but the dreary rules of everyday society—like schooling and manners and stiff clothes. Huck's idea of liberty is the freedom not to wear shoes.

After a particularly terrifying imprisonment by his father, Huck escapes his home, discovers a raft on an island in the Mississippi River, and determines to drift away—to Freedom. Fate even provides him with a companion: Jim, an escaped slave who is fleeing from the ownership of the very family that had sought to help Huck by civilizing him with education, religion, regular meals, and clean sheets.

Together, the two of them set off on the greatest of adventures any two people could take—toward the Freedom of the human soul.

They encounter the best and the worst of people. They find storms and sunrises and billions of stars sailing overhead as they float down the mightiest of American rivers. And then it happens—the greatest single scene in literature.

They are nearing the Free States, where Jim, by law, can no longer be considered another man's property. Jim begins to speculate on what Freedom will mean.

And Jim, mind you, is not remotely an idealized example born of political correctness; he is superstitious, uneducated, sometimes pompous—a comedic caricature, yet one so distinctive and real that he grabs the reader by the throat. He tells Huck that once he is free, he will go to work right away, and now, instead of his money going to the "massah," he will save every penny and collect enough money, even if it takes years, to go back and buy his wife's freedom. And if the owners won't sell his wife, then he'll hire an Abolitionist to go steal her back! Then he and his wife will set to work to earn enough money to buy their children's freedom. And if the owners won't sell them, then they'll steal them back too!

Huck recounts, in the first-person voice of the novel, "It froze me to hear such terrible talk!" For Huck has been taught, in his schooling by God-fearing people who tried to rescue Huck from savagery, that slaves are in their rightful place, and Abolitionists were the lowest form of humanity—humanity being a designation that apparently did not include those born into bondage.

Again, it is important to remember that the people who legally owned Jim had many layers of goodness. They were perhaps kinder to their slaves than most slave owners were; they, among all the other God-fearing folks of their community, were willing to brave the chaos brought into their lives by adopting Huck, and they gave him the best they had, as well as they understood the best to be.

No one in *Huckleberry Finn* is perfect, least of all Huck himself. And he recognizes that what he is facing is a crisis of epic proportions, a choice that will mark Life and Death—not just Jim's but also his own.

Huck knows—*knows*! Because he has been taught by good and righteous people that anyone who helps a slave escape his rightful owners is going to Hell.

So Huck resolves to do the only sane and proper thing: he will take a canoe, under cover of darkness—and the cover of the lie he tells Jim, that he is going to scout out their whereabouts so they'll be sure they are safe—go to one of the villages on the shore, and rouse good men from their beds to come back and capture Jim so he can be returned to his rightful owners, where he belongs.

Huck shoves off from the raft, assisted with a push from Jim, who tells him tenderly to take care to keep himself safe. Huck rows out under a burden of remorse and then hears Jim's heartfelt sigh and his soft words carried over the quiet surface of the water: "Dah you goes, de ole true Huck; de on'y white genlman dat ever kep' his promise to ole Jim."

And Huck has that greatest of moments: a change of heart. And to be faithful to that new heart, Huck Finn was willing to go to Hell.

Huck Finn was an outlaw. At that moment he became a True Outlaw, not just a boy whose status as a fugitive from adoption, even from civilization itself, gave the authorities all the justification they wanted to force him into their way of life. Something new happened to Huck: a Revelation—brought forth by a slave's loving gratitude, showing he was not an object to be owned, but a man to be free—and a Transformation, one that defied every rational assumption of Huck's previous life.

And suddenly—I understood at fifteen, and I understand now—Huck was alive, alive in such a way that his old life could not be considered life at all but a kind of walking death from which he was suddenly awakened.

The *new* life was not without its confusions or its struggles and missteps. But it was a life that would not permit his return to prejudice and ignorance. He was awake and could not go back to sleep.

Huckleberry Finn is a great story. When I first encountered the tale of William Wallace, I had the sense that it, too, might have the Power to awaken, to call a man into Life. And I wasn't thinking so much of what it would do to others but what it would do to me. *Braveheart* was the story that I needed to hear.

We live in an age when Religion connotes something dark, even hateful, and this assumption of negativity is prevalent not just on the trendy television shows where satirists mock rules and dogma as if they had none of their own. I have heard pastors of popular churches close their sermons by inviting people "not into Religion but into relationship." And, of course, this rises from their honest desire to separate love from legalism.

But many who rage against religious rules have made new rules of their own: the *Huckleberry Finn* that Mark Twain wrote has been banned from schools, either outlawed outright or censored into a version meant to spare children from harsh truths.

It is a harsh truth that prejudice and racist epithets exist. It is also a harsh truth that a boy like Huck, the epitome of White Trash, can come to see in one he has ridiculed, tormented, and disparaged not only another human being but also a brother.

It is the essence of harsh truths that the initial response to Jesus—who preached the inclusiveness of the Creator's Love—was, is, and always will be to distrust him. The preaching isn't the problem. He made claims. For these they killed him. We all did. We all do. He was killed by those who considered themselves the keepers of Order, the guardians of True Faith, the keepers of Rules.

The troublesome claim hinges on the massive difference between *a* and *the*. Had Jesus said he was *a* child of God, no one would have cared. He made a different claim. Confronting what he meant by that claim requires the daring of an outlaw.

To me, Religion is what you believe *outside* of the law—what you believe because you know what it is to step beyond the rationalizations, to move away from the rules and codes and habits that keep you asleep, to leap toward the terrifying unknown. Into Life.

TWENTY-FIVE

JUMPING JACK FLASH

I HAVE A FRIEND WHOSE FATHER WAS MAFIA. NOT *IN* THE Mafia, he *was* the Mafia—the godfather of one of the Five Families of New York, in the good/bad old days of the 1960s. They went to a lot of funerals, many that his father had known were going to happen before the guy in the coffin did.

Like Michael Corleone in *The Godfather* movie, my friend—let's call him Frank—is brilliant with strong ideals, and like the movie version of himself, his father did not want him in the family business. But young Frank's inherent genius for seeing the ways human motives and weaknesses weave themselves into inevitable outcomes made him a natural candidate to become the greatest of all Mafia leaders.

When he was a boy, in about 1967, the Rolling Stones were coming to New York City. My friend—this was many years before I met him, but he shared with me this story—loved music, and due to some family connections, he found himself with tickets. On the front row.

He didn't really know much about the Rolling Stones then, just that they were another of the British bands that were popping up everywhere, sporting odd haircuts and odder accents, trying to sound like black blues or white rockabilly singers, all of them from the South. He went because he had the tickets, he was a teenager, and it was somewhere to go.

He told me, "They came out on the stage. They played the opening riff of 'Jumping Jack Flash.' And my life changed forever."

Young Frank did not become a leader of the Mafia; he went to California and became massively successful in Hollywood. His gift of plotting turned to creating entertainment. Along the way he taught me quite a bit about writing.

I grew up in Tennessee and in Virginia. My Father was not a Mafia chieftain, but in his own way he was a lion. He was also a Baptist deacon, and in my youth I was taken, not willingly, to an endless stream of church services and tent revivals. I've seen many people walk down an aisle in surrender to salvation.

I know full well that those outside this experience consider it a self-deception, but the sudden redirection of a life has happened too many times, in too many contexts, and to too many people to dismiss all conversion as fraud.

But the change in my friend's life—a Transformation I recognized and accepted as surely as I accepted the sincerity of those who wept for their sins in churches—had not come in a cathedral, where a choir sang the "Hallelujah Chorus" or in a tent, where farmers sang "The Old Rugged Cross."

The Rolling Stones played "Jumping Jack Flash" and Frank was called to new possibilities; he was picked up and hurled outside the old rules into creativity. Into Life.

I believe God uses everything—whatever God wants to use—to open doors for us and to urge us through them.

But we're human. The moment we step into the new territory, we start wanting to control our journey and our destination. We want to set ourselves up as God. We start making rules and insist they be treated as commandments, the only way to God.

TWENTY-SIX

MILANO

A FEW YEARS AGO MY ASSISTANT CAME INTO MY OFFICE AND said, "We got an interesting request you might want to look at."

I call them "assistants," since that's what people say these days, but the young people who work in an office, covering phone calls and correspondence, are more like apprentices. In my Father's day these people were secretaries and were often older, with more experience than the boss. Having a good one was like the young officer in a combat regiment with a hardened sergeant who, theoretically, was below him in the chain of command but who could steer him in the right direction.

My assistant had received an invitation for me to speak. Now, as you can guess, I love speaking. I love telling stories and love telling them before a live audience. It's in my nature. I'm like the hound dog named Trusty in the Disney feature-length cartoon *Lady and the Tramp* who's always drawling to the other dogs: "Ah don't recollect if I've told y'all the story about . . ."

Most speaking engagements that are proposed to me are events I don't want to do because they involve travel and I like to be at home, so most requests for them don't even get by my assistant.

This one was different. "It's in Milan, Italy," my assistant said. "At the Catholic University of Milan."

I have to tell you, I love me some Italy.

I read the letter of invitation, and it was beautifully written; the language was fragrant with an elegance of manners and grace. The writer mentioned that he had begun a program to help young people learn not just the mechanics of telling stories through film but also the deeper pathways of the spirit and the heart.

I wanted to go. But I was lonely in my life, in that crushing loneliness you feel when you're eating alone and wishing you had somebody to talk to, even if it was to say, "Ah don't recollect I've told you the story about . . ."

Bob from Afghanistan had recently broken up with a woman he had dated for years and had even struggled to marry. He was feeling the same hole in his life that I was feeling after divorce. So I asked him if he'd like to go with me; we'd even stop over in Paris, two Wild and Crazy Guys cruising for French women. He said yes right away. And off we headed for Europe.

The man who set up the trip and had written the invitation was named Armando Fumagalli.

Armando is a member of Opus Dei, a Catholic order begun by a Spanish priest who saw a need for spiritual and physical self-discipline in the modern world. The author of *The Da Vinci Code* took advantage of the privacy of this order to make members of the order the villains in writing his fantasies about history.

I HAVE TO STOP HERE FOR A MOMENT AND COMMENT ON *HISTORY*.

I've done four films in a row for which I could draw on the eyewitness accounts of actual participants in the events portrayed. Oddly enough, it was *Braveheart*, set seven hundred years in the past, that raised the eyebrows and twisted the knickers of many academics who consider themselves historians.

I don't mean to disparage historians; what I want to do is make a distinction between lovers of history and lovers of statistics. By *history* I mean the past alive in the present, when a person with a heartbeat walks a battlefield and feels within his chest the heartbeats of the men who struggled there; when we look at an ancient gown and feel the rhythm of the waltzing; when a person stands in the spot where William Wallace stood and heard his death sentence, and looks up at the window above him, as I did, and feels the reality of that moment—not the numbers of judges or buttons on their clothes, but what it must've felt like to be him, *there*. That is history to me, and some who teach it have that love.

During the making of *We Were Soldiers*, I met a young man who was a captain in the Marine Corps Reserves. When the Gulf War began, he was called up to lead a Marine Recon company. They were, as the Marines say, "the point of the spear." I saw him when he returned home and was on his way to Yale to earn a master's degree in history. He told me that his experiences in the war had caused him to reevaluate all his notions about history.

"Once," he said, "I heard firing break out all across our front line. I ran to the perimeter to see what was happening, and nothing was out there. I asked the men what they were firing at. One swore they were being attacked by infantry; another said he saw tanks; another said he saw planes. This was in the desert—they could see for miles. And there was *nothing* there. But every man swore he saw something.

"And if it's like that," he went on, "at an event where I was physically present, how much can I trust accounts that were filtered and processed by people who were nowhere near the battlefield?"

We project our own prejudices and desires onto everything we see. Two people watch the same presidential debate and make entirely different decisions—at least publically—about which candidate made the other look dim-witted.

Bill Nack, who wrote the definitive book on Secretariat, also cov-ered boxing for *Sports Illustrated*, and I once asked him to explain for me the broad disparities in the judging of boxing matches. He didn't deny that corruption could exist, but he highlighted the human factor: "You tend to watch the boxer that you like," he told me. "So you see him throw punches, and you see them land; you tend to miss the punches that are thrown back at him, and to discount their effectiveness."

All that is one thing, but fuzzy logic is another. I've heard people state as absolute fact the nonsense that some fiction writer—or a fiction writer who is pretending to write nonfiction—has made up. The same people who insist we should listen to scientists on one subject will completely discount a scientific approach when it supports their own prejudice.

It takes about an hour to read the Gospel According to Mark—scarcely more than a pamphlet, and the most influential book ever written—and people condemn Christianity and say it is nonsense with-out ever having read the sixteen chapters that encompass its essence. Others bring up supposedly hidden gospels that were suppressed by the Catholic Church and were allegedly written by gnostics or others at the time of the earliest gospels. This is bunk, and credible biblical scholars know it.

A comparable theory is the one that says William Shakespeare was a fraud and not the author of the plays and poems that bear his name. Conspiracy lovers get sucked right into this notion, discounting the fact that absolutely no one at the time the works were written ever suggested that anyone except Shakespeare of Avon could possibly be the author. The whole notion was concocted early in the 1900s, more than three hundred years later.

All of which brings us back to Jesus, and Da Vinci, and *The Da Vinci Code*, and Opus Dei, and my acquaintance with Armando, one of Opus Dei's members.

SHORTLY AFTER BOB FROM AFGHANISTAN AND I LANDED IN Milan, a tall man with curly black hair, a scholar's eyes, and an impish smile met us. This was Armando Fumagalli. He was not shy so much as he was gentle. Gentle is an interesting concept to me. Weak is weak, but gentle is not weak. Something about this guy was strong; there was a certainty about him and a playfulness. I don't know how else to describe it.

I taught the first day of class and loved the students. They laughed more than American students did; this surprised me.

On the second day Armando offered to guide Bob and me to some of the sights of Milano. The artisans of Italy had just completed a thorough cleaning of Da Vinci's crowning fresco, *The Last Supper*; would we care to see it?

We jumped at the chance. Class ended midafternoon, and we arrived at the building housing the fresco just after four. And there we were, all surprised to learn that the exhibit closed at four. We couldn't go in.

Bob and I were cursing under our breath—at least I was. We were leaving early the next day, and it looked as if we'd missed our chance to see one of the greatest artworks in history at a time when it was just restored to its original glory. Armando was unfazed. "Let me see what I can do," he said.

He strolled to the guard at the door, spoke a few quiet words, and waved us over. "It is no problem," he said. "We can go in."

"This guy knows the pope," I whispered to Bob.

We entered and stood before Da Vinci's masterpiece. It leapt off the wall at us. The three of us, just us, drifting through the space, looking up from different angles, taking it all in.

It qualified as a religious experience. I had no idea that it could get even better.

When we left, the sun was drifting down, and I felt a deep calm. I believe we all did. "What else might you wish to see?" Armando asked, in his perfect Italian-accented English.

"Are there any nice churches we could look into?" I asked. "I like to see what people have constructed as their sacred spaces."

Armando thought a moment and said, "There is a good one nearby. We can walk."

He led us into a sanctuary that took my breath. The building was less ornate than I'd imagined it would be, here in the home of the Renaissance. In fact, it was surprisingly simple. The empty spaces were what I noticed, the vast openness between the white walls. But they were *not* empty; they were filled with an intention, an invitation, an inspiration.

Elderly ladies moved down the aisles on their knees, cleaning the floor with small brushes. A few people were scattered in the pews, praying or meditating.

We stood in the back—an Opus Dei Catholic, a former Muslim, a Protestant. All of us silent. And then I asked Armando, "Would it be all right if we prayed?" I didn't know if it would somehow be improper—un-Catholic, un-Italian, un-something.

Armando shrugged. "Of course."

I looked at Bob. "Would you want to pray—or not to?" I whispered.

"No," he surprised me by saying, "I would pray."

So we knelt, the three of us, and prayed side by side, in silence.

That night Bob and I were having dinner. We talked about women and money and life. Guy things. And then I said, "I don't want to invade your privacy. But would you mind telling me what you prayed?"

"I don't mind telling you, Beeg Guy. I thanked God that there were people who would build a place so beautiful—and people who would keep it beautiful."

There we have a picture and a question. A Catholic, a Protestant, and a former Muslim have all knelt together to pray.

Two would call themselves Christians; one would not.

But would Jesus recognize all three and call them Brothers?

I believe you know my answer. What is yours?

TWENTY-SEVEN

LIVING THE BRAVEHEART LIFE

IT IS ONE THING TO TALK OR WRITE ABOUT IT—AND ANOTHER thing to live it.

Yet here is another paradox: for me, talking and writing about it have been part of living the Braveheart Life. In communicating with each other—and I mean *truly* communicating, both talking and listening—we open ourselves to the possibility of the experience of the presence of Life beyond anything we have known—what we Christians call the Holy Spirit.

What I just said could leave some, especially those who come from the same traditions I grew up in, to ask if I'm saying that the Holy Spirit could be called or known by other names.

I think that is a question best answered not by me but by the One they are really asking the question of. Ask God. Ask the Holy Spirit, wherever it is you feel that Presence you recognize. I'm not trying to be obscure—I'm trying to be quite clear: I mean to literally get on your knees and say to what may feel like nothingness or emptiness, or may feel divine: Are you the Holy Spirit? Are you God? Is Jesus your Son?

You will be surprised.

LIVING AND SHARING

It must be clear by now that when I speak of the Braveheart Life and the way that, for me, it is so identified with the Life that is Christ, I am speaking of an experience, not an understanding or an intellectual argument.

I am not trying to avoid understanding or the intellect that gropes its way in circles in hopes of grasping concepts. But to me, that is what intellect does: it moves in circles and never really gets anywhere.

Experience is profound and transforming; experience is growth. But experience is difficult to share. The Father, the Teacher, the Warrior, and even the Sage all discover that the Braveheart Life is a personal journey. "Yea, though I walk through the valley of the shadow of death . . . thy rod and thy staff they comfort me."[1] When King David wrote this psalm three thousand years ago, he said "I" and "me" instead of "we" and "us." He was a Father, a Teacher, a Warrior, and a Sage; he was king of his nation. And still he knew that the deepest aspects of his life were between God and himself.

If experience cannot be passed along, can it still be shared?

Yes, it can.

We may not be able to explain an experience; we can use adjectives, such as *transformational* or *transcendent* or even *awesome* and *wonderful*. To anyone outside the experience, these fluffy words mean nothing. Testimonies of the Power of an experience may make someone else curious or envious, but they bring them no closer to its Truth.

And yet there is a medium—a tool, a weapon, if you will—for sharing an experience.

That medium is Love.

Love, and only Love, has the Power to transform.

I pause as I write this and reflect that miserable people certainly have the potency to make others miserable, and that all of us, when we feel fear and hate, can allow those feelings to spread. My understanding—I grope with the intellectual circles, just as others do—is that the darker elements of life are part of our nature.

But Love lifts us and brings us into contact with a higher nature, the nature of God. There is an element of choice in Love, and it seems to me that it is greater than choice. We choose to listen to it, to obey it—or we don't.

Loving God has a similarity, at least in this aspect, to falling in love. It happens. We can wish we were in love; we can believe we will never know love again . . . and it comes upon us and takes over. Romeo is telling his friends how crushed his heart is, how it is dead, when he sees Juliet and all those other feelings and illusions fly away. God can come upon us. We speak of seeking God. But God is always seeking us.

I don't know how or even why this is true; I only know that it is true.

SEVERAL TIMES IN MY LIFE I'VE THOUGHT ABOUT TRYING TO write about all this: my family and my calling. Why have I waited? What has prevented me? Another way to ask this question is, who is the enemy?

"If God be for us, who can be against us?"[2]

In the kabbalah tradition of Judaism, they speak of the yetzer hara—the Resistance. Could we call that the Resister? In the experience of it, it is profoundly personal.

Kyle, one of my friends in Mississippi who is also a publisher, told me he thought such a book was a "sunset book," one an author writes at the close of his career. I didn't like the thought of that. I hope I never run out of something I want to say.

Yet where does that feeling come from? Is it pride? C. S. Lewis wrote that Pride is the dominant sin; other sins come from the unhealthy excess of an impulse that is healthy when kept in its place: hunger, ambition, sexual desires, and thrift can all be good things, until they turn into gluttony, envy, lust, and greed. But Pride, Lewis tells us, is straight from Hell. It is the desire to be better than others.

Before I ever read Dr. Lewis's work, it occurred to me that perhaps the Original Sin was the desire to matter. We offer our hand to God; whether God uses it, whether his hand becomes ours, is up to him.

I've heard a number of Christians say they've promised God that if they can rise to prominence in the entertainment business, then they will give God all the glory. I'm not sure that this isn't much different from the football player who scores a touchdown and then points upward, or the baseball player who points toward Heaven when he finishes circling the bases after hitting a home run.

Of course, Jesus didn't say, "If I lift you up, draw all men to me." He said, "I, if I be lifted up . . . will draw all men unto me."[3] How we, who seek to follow Christ, actually lift him up instead of ourselves is one of the great questions of living a Braveheart Life.

And that brings me to a crucial point: *the heart that is brave is not ours; it is God's.*

I think Jesus meant this, even about himself. He identified himself with God; I have friends who want to deny this because they want to make Jesus more palatable to others, but this flies in the face of facts. If Jesus did not identify himself with God, then why was he crucified?

The better question is, what did he mean when he said, "I am the way, the truth, and the life: no man cometh unto the Father, but by me"?[4]

I've always believed Jesus said exactly that. It's exactly why I have believed him, and believed in him. I haven't always been able to explain what I think he meant, but I realize all I'll ever do is just that: try to explain what I *think* he meant. The experience of what he means with that statement is something else.

A DEVOTIONAL LIFE

As I've mentioned, I grew up a Baptist, and Baptists love the Bible. I still do what I did as a boy; just before I turn out the lights and say my last prayer, I read some passage, usually from the Gospels.

The prayer I say is not rigid, though I often pray for the same people.

In the morning it's different. When I wake, I tend to pray the same words; they are personal, and I see no reason to share them here. But I will share what I pray—exactly what I pray—each morning before I begin to write. I'm not suggesting the words have a power to themselves. But people have shared their prayers with me, and in that sharing there is power.

> Oh Lord. Thank you for this work. I pray you bless me in it and others through it, however it is your will.
>
> I pray to offer it to you as you offer it to me—in love and in faith and in hope.
>
> I pray that you would bless me, bless me indeed, increase my territory; that thy hand be upon me to keep me from evil and that I cause no pain.
>
> I thank you that you are God Almighty, Lord of all creation; that your creativity is without limit, and I am part of your creativity. Thy will be done. For this I give thanks, and rejoice, in Jesus' name. Amen.

WHEN I AM IN A ROUGH PATCH, I OFTEN FIND RELIEF IN TAK-ing a long walk and reciting a collection of affirmations that I wrote for myself, inspired by a friend who had made a permanent change in her own life—she had lost an enormous amount of weight and had kept it off. I asked her how, and she told me she'd written down things that she wanted to be true, and she said them to herself each day as if they were true. Here are mine:

- I live in the present. The past and future are not now. The past does not define me, and the future whispers of possibilities that have reality only in the now of my life. I am, at this moment, exactly where God wants me to be.
- I am free from guilt. I do not blame others, and I do not accept blame from others. I am free of guilt.
- I accept the love of God. I know God loves me, no matter who else does or doesn't.
- When I find myself repeating a pattern that I recognize leads to destruction and despair, I seek to change that habit into something that leads in the direction of Life and Love, and in the very seeking I am finding.
- When I find myself suffering in confusion and despair, I remind myself that God uses my doubt and my delight, my pain and my pleasure, all for his purposes, and in his own time.
- When I find myself frustrated with feelings of failure, I remember that God finds ways to teach me, even when— perhaps especially when—I am lost.
- I know that God knows what I can't know; he sees what I can't see, and does what I can't do. For this I give thanks, and rejoice in Jesus' name. Amen.

Once in a while I have added to this. A few years ago I added this statement:

- I know that the voice that tells me I am not made to be loved is not the voice of God. I believe—and trust that it is stronger to believe than to know—that God's deepest desire is that I feel joy and peace and especially love; in fact, God wants me to be loved and to love so much that I can best understand God by saying that God *is* Love. In this I rejoice, in Love.

And is it stronger to believe than to know?
Of course it is.

TWENTY-EIGHT

WHERE DO YOU PUT YOUR GUNS?

WHEN *BRAVEHEART* WAS STILL IN THE FILMING STAGE, I GOT a phone call from executives at another movie studio. They wanted me to fly to Hawaii to meet Kevin Costner, who had read the script for *Braveheart* and wanted to talk with me about any other ideas I might have.

Because the trip was a long one, I went to a bookstore, and in the history section I found a work with the captivating title, *We Were Soldiers Once . . . and Young.* I bought it and began reading the book on the plane. In the prologue I came across this declaration: "Hollywood got it wrong every . . . time, whetting twisted political knives on the bones of our dead brothers."[1] I was hooked.

When I got off the plane, I called my agent.

Eventually I would find myself ready to direct the movie *We Were Soldiers*—only I wasn't ready. I had never served in the military. At one point during my college years, I had planned to join the Platoon Leaders Class of the US Marine Corps, but the tragedies at My Lai and the loss of political leadership and the honor culture surrounding our involvement in Vietnam had soured me on such intentions. I ultimately experienced a draft physical that was one of the most depressing experiences in waste and mindless bureaucracy I had ever experienced.

187

But I respected the men who had gone into the hell that was Vietnam, and I was fascinated to see that for many of them it wasn't hell—or more accurately, that it was an experience of both horrific terror and profound Brotherhood. It was my longing to learn all I could about both that led me to Ranger School.

One of the exercises there was in combat leadership situations. A Ranger would be given a problem, and one of the questions he would have to resolve would be where to put his firepower. And there was no single right answer; there were many answers. But the conclusion of whether it was a correct placement depended on other factors.

What I take from this is that right courses can't be predicted or pre-chosen. You have to choose when the outcome is not only unknown but also unknowable.

And that means the Leader never quits influencing the situation.

There were many amazing things about Rangers, to me. One was that unlike everything I'd seen or read about other elite fighting forces—who call the trainees who wish to be a part of their culture names like maggot (or worse)—those who enter Ranger School are called Ranger from the first day. Every man who comes to the school (including me, in fact) has passed fitness tests that prove he has the physical capacity to do everything they require. So at Ranger School there is an implied assumption: you can do this; now the question is, do you really want to? As long as you want to, we will train you and call you Ranger. When you cease to want to, you may go freely, and only then will we cease to call you Ranger.

Rangers are known by the motto "Rangers lead the way." There are many ideals taught by the Rangers—resilience, the ability to think and perform under stress, loyalty to each other, and a refusal to leave another behind, ever—and all of these values are consequences of the Rangers' central purpose: leadership.

In one of the leadership exercises, a Ranger who is designated to serve as leader for the moment (in Ranger School none of the students wear rank; in a given hour a sergeant may be given leadership authority over lieutenants and captains in his training group) is thrown into a desperate scenario: Half your men are wounded and screaming for help; you are surrounded and nearly out of ammunition and water. You have only one heavy weapon that is still functioning . . . and you are lost. You have no idea where the enemy is, and worst of all, you have no idea how long it will be before your own allies can come to you. What do you do?

What the instructors at Ranger School are looking for is a leader who turns to his few remaining men and says, "Everybody calm down! *You*, stick your fingers into that guy's wounds and make him stop screaming. *You*, run back to our lines and bring back all the ammunition you can carry, as fast as you can go. And *you*, help me set up this machine gun! We're gonna kill every enemy that comes down that road! *Now!*"

That attitude is the initial quality they seek to teach, but it isn't the last. The next important question is, where do you put your guns?

And here's the part that struck me: There is no single right answer. Each of the instructors has his own idea of where the optimal strategic placement of the machine gun would be; they don't all agree where that is. And while I was at Ranger School, a trainee from Poland (at Fort Benning, America's allies are offered the same elite warrior education that the army's best men get—and there are Navy SEALs and special forces from other branches there as well) chose to place his primary weapon in a position that none of the instructors thought to be proper, but when that surprising choice proved to be effective, the instructors awarded the Pole the highest grade on the exercise. Originality is a highly valued quality in a Ranger leader.

I've wondered when I would get around to saying this, and now here it is: I place my guns with Jesus.

What do I mean by that?

Like the young men who are learning to be Rangers, every one of u' in life has problems that are immediate. The wounded are screaming—and most likely, *we* are the wounded. We are down to so few resources of help that it seems we have none at all. We are lost and so is everyone around us, and we all want to be shouting mindlessly and staring at the world and at each other with wild, vacant eyes.

The decision a young Rangers makes is not one of education or experience. In a certain way it is a decision of Faith. It is the choice of action over Fear, the choice of Life over Death.

That is why I choose Jesus.

Forget everything you think you've been told about Jesus for a moment and assume that I'm not trying to convince you of anything beyond the truth of my own experience. I don't want your money. I don't want your mind—all that is yours to do with as you will. And as for your soul, if you believe you have one . . . well, that is something else again. Maybe your soul, in a sense, is mine, just as mine is yours. If we have a soul, if we are all souls, then all our souls are God's.

I have watched three sons being born—my own sons, if any child can be called "our own." To see a child enter the world is an experience of profound mystery, as well as majesty. It is joyful, but not in the same straightforward sense as the pure excitement of seeing a loved one enter the door unexpectedly. A birth has qualities of awe and even fear mingled with relief and sadness, along with all happiness. Charles Dickens is one of my favorite writers, and I once found a congratulatory birth card that carried this quote attributed to him: "I love these little ones, and it is no small thing when they, who are so fresh from God, love us."

Birth is not the only time in life when such experiences combine. They are present in Death too.

I was with my Mother last year when the final few gasps of air were leaving her body. I was not with her for the last one; she took that one just before I walked back into her room. It was a terrible experience, and yet it was beautiful. I looked at the body on the bed—and it was not my Mother. It was a body. It was a vessel that she had infused, but it was no longer her. My Mother's spirit was Somewhere; she was with God.

You may call that something else—the Universe, Spirit, whatever. What matters, I think, is what you mean when you choose that name.

I feel a bond with Christians because I imagine that when they say "Jesus" and "the Christ," they mean the same Son of the same God that I do—though, of course, that is by no means a reliable assumption. I can't be responsible for what others mean; I can speak only for myself.

While in seminary I heard that the great theologian Karl Barth once asserted that it is meaningless to say you believe in God unless you can say what God you mean. Saying it is difficult; sometimes we just have to point to a picture or a story.

I point to the crucifixion.

I choose Jesus because Jesus has chosen me. He has chosen all of us.

TWENTY-NINE

So Who Goes to Heaven?

I cannot write about Christianity and my own personal belief in Jesus without pausing at least a moment to talk about empathy. Whenever I speak of my deepest values, something in me wants to try to step across into the other person's shoes and listen from their perspective.

It seems to me that whoever is bound for Heaven would possess a willingness to appreciate the honest struggles, strengths, and limitations of everyone else; otherwise, Heaven would not be a heaven at all. And here is the point: I am not the judge of who goes to Heaven—and neither are you. Thank Heaven for that! If I were the judge, I would be casting pretty much everybody, including myself, into Hell. Beneath the surface of the love and tolerance that I try to project, I am a self-righteous, judgmental, and unforgiving human being. I pray to be different, but in my heart of hearts, I know my prayers aren't completely sincere—and that's why I have to pray them! As C. S. Lewis said, "No man who says *I'm as good as you* believes it."[1] And if we truly forgave other people their trespasses against us, we wouldn't have to keep saying the prayer.

None of us deserve Heaven.

But God has given us Life.

And Jesus came along to show us who God is and who *we* are.

When the *Passion of the Christ* movie was being made, a controversy arose around the world, based on the assertion that this version of the story, told with as much commitment to be faithful to the original story as any Passion play ever told, argued that Jews were responsible for the killing of Jesus. A deeply intelligent and thoughtful Jewish friend of mine saw the movie and told me, "I am not a religious man, but I'm Jewish by family and tradition, and I thought that film was the vilest piece of Jew-hating I ever saw. I couldn't believe that crowds didn't come boiling out of that theater and cause massive violence against us."

I said to him, "Since millions of people around the world saw the movie, and not one single act of violent anti-Semitism was attributed to it, doesn't that make you think? Christians didn't take that story as saying Jews killed Jesus; we believe all of us did." My son Andrew was my strongest example of this reaction. He, like millions of people, found himself shattered as he watched Jesus' crucifixion, in grief at what an innocent man—in our belief the only innocent man—had suffered because of *him*.

The great thing about this is that in the end, to you it doesn't matter what my son or I or Mel Gibson or one of my Jewish friends believes. To you it only matters what *you* believe.

And none of the explanations of any faith will make sense to you if you are not sincerely open to an experience with God. That is both the hardest and the easiest thing in the world. It's hard because we can't compel God to do anything, and we humans generally begin learning that lesson as we first start trying to draw God into our own desires and agenda.

Christians, since the beginning of the faith, have tried to explain their beliefs to others, and while billions have believed, other billions haven't.

I am not going to change that fact. That won't stop me from believing what I believe, and you, since you are reading this, will know that you won't change it either because this is how each of us is made.

OUTLAW CHRISTIANITY

One Christmas I found myself writing a verse that pretty
conveys how I see Christianity:

A Poor Girl's Child

Long ago and far away, a poor girl's child was born
Shepherds watched all through the night,
    and kings came Christmas morn
A distant angel dressed in white said, "Jesus is his name."
And since that dark, cold, lonely night,
    the world was not the same.

He grew to tell us, "God is love, so love your fellow man."
He said a child could come to God—that anybody can.
Though human hearts grew cruel and
    cold, his soul was not for sale
To his birth we brought him gold
And to his death, a nail.

And so we hung him to a cross, and filled God's heart with pain
Yet in his dying, death was lost, and it was life we gained
And when they put him in the ground
    they swore that he was dead
Those who knew him swore he lives. They
    died for what they said.

Long ago and far away, a poor girl's child was born
Shepherds watched all through the night
And kings came Christmas morn.
So if you ask me why I cry, and bow my knees to him
It's because I cope through Jesus' hope,
    and see God's face in him.[2]

AND THIS BRINGS ME START TO FINISH—AND FINISH BACK TO start. When we look at a sky that is flushed with rose and yellow, we are looking at either a sunrise or a sunset. You may say that which one it is, is simply a matter of fact; if I can tell you what time of day it is, then you will know whether day is coming, or night.

Both are coming, of course, one after another. Do we love the light or the darkness? I know—know from my own experience and know also from faith that isn't exactly connected to experience—that God can speak to us through either.

We are born. We die. Is one of them sunrise and the other sunset? If so, which is which?

How you answer those questions makes all the difference in the world. Not to me—I have to make my own choice—but to you.

PART VI

VICTORY

THIRTY

LOVE TRANSFORMS

WILLIAM WALLACE, IN *BRAVEHEART*, IS BETRAYED BY THE nobles of Scotland, and in the legends surrounding William Wallace— at least according to the guard at Edinburgh Castle who first told me some of those legends—even Robert the Bruce is somehow implicated.

It was obvious to me that if the historical facts really went this way, then the man I've always imagined was my ancestor—and therefore, in the reasoning of my soul, like me—had to have felt a staggering sense of betrayal. One of the most shocking and powerful scenes in the movie is the scene on the battlefield when Wallace rips the helmet off a man sent by Edward Longshanks to kill him and discovers it is Robert the Bruce himself; the pain Mel Gibson portrayed in that moment is something everyone in the audience recognized—and could relate to.

Every human being knows what it feels like to be betrayed, and I believe we all know what it feels like to betray. The awful experience of having chosen the wrong course through fear, greed, lust, or any of our other natural weaknesses is made far worse by the realization that in doing so we have left someone else in a terrible situation. The feeling that we have been betrayed ourselves may feel even worse, though it would be hard to say that it's worse to be the betrayed than to be the betrayer.

In either case, part of what betrayal generates is a profound aloneness. To be betrayed is to be left Alone. But as Robert the Bruce discovers in *Braveheart*, betraying produces the same isolation.

William Wallace suffers because of the betrayal of Robert the Bruce and the other Scottish nobles. All of his hopes are shattered; all of his efforts—or so it seems at the moment—become dust. Many of his friends have died because of the betrayal, along with many more of the people Wallace had inspired in the struggle for Freedom.

As I reflect on this now, part of the heroic journey William Wallace makes in *Braveheart* is to experience exactly such a horror. Freedom means taking risks and facing at least the possibility of such betrayal, if not the full reality of it. A slave remains in bondage always, but the free person risks betrayal.

Nowhere does this dynamic leap out more forcefully than in relationships of the heart. We think of the single person as free and speak of marriage as if it is the surrender of freedom, but surely marriage could offer a new and greater level of freedom, the kind that comes with companionship and confidence and commitment.

But it also brings the possibility of betrayal.

When I was in a college writing class, the professor asked us freshmen to write down what we thought was the greatest betrayal. Most of us imagined that it would be the betrayal of adultery. Our teacher said he thought it was not the sexual infidelity of one partner in a relationship but rather their suicide because it was the abandonment without any possibility of a discussion about why.

William Wallace is betrayed. He feels the devastation of it. He feels the anger, surely, because after a time of reflection he returns in retribution and vengeance.

If the story ended there, it would be typical of most tales. I once was on a plane trip with a man who had headed several Hollywood studios and had become a prominent producer. He was a fascinating and in many ways delightful rogue. On that trip he said, "You wanna know what a story is? I'll tell ya! Somebody kills something you love—your wife, your kid, your dog. Then you kill him! Now *that's* a *story!*" Most Hollywood stories are that and little else.

But some stories explore what growth is, and I believe *Braveheart* does. William Wallace realizes that he can keep fighting forever and that he may win some battles and may lose some, but nothing fundamental will change. He must change himself, and he must get others to change.

If you know the story of Jesus, does this sound familiar?

Jesus taught his disciples for three years. He chose them, lived with them, and showed them everything possible to show: miracles, lessons, visions. He told them what would happen, and the future unfolded exactly as he foretold. And yet, at the ultimate moment, all of them betrayed him.

I had wondered before, and as I wrote *Braveheart* I wondered again, whether Jesus had any sort of spiritual crisis as he realized the disciples would betray him. He *knew* they would; he told Peter to his face that he would become an utter coward and deny three times that he even knew Jesus after Peter boldly, and apparently courageously, declared that he would never abandon Jesus—yet at the time that it mattered, Peter did exactly that.

Jesus knew who Peter was and how he was. And Jesus knew who *he* was.

Jesus knew that Transformation is possible.

I believe that's what we have to remember when we experience betrayal—from either side.

A friend of mine recently went through a horrible divorce. Her husband became violent and vengeful, though by everything that anyone knew, he was the one who deserved anger and banishment. He accused his wife of all the things she was innocent of but he had done himself. He was a lawyer and used the court system to attack her repeatedly, even though each time the courts ruled in her favor.

Recently he tried again to use the courts against her, and she was facing an awful trial. I suggested that there might be something good in the process, and she looked at me as if I had gone insane.

I told her the experience might allow her to transform. When a relationship falls apart, we feel savage guilt. In her case the guilt involved the sense of responsibility of having chosen the wrong person. My hope was that the awful experience of seeing her husband's full hatred would bring her to the Transformation of letting go of the baggage she carried.

Love transforms.

THIRTY-ONE

EGO

WE TALK ABOUT SELF-DENIAL. JESUS SAID THAT TO FIND Heaven a man must "deny himself . . . and follow me."[1] Anyone who wrestles with issues of faith or approaches life with a psychological point of view, or for that matter enters into deep relationships, gropes with the issues of Self. And to live a Braveheart Life, one must ask, "Who am I?"

For me, the question of Identity has been central in the journey of my whole life. As I've already described, I was seeking to learn about my ancestry—certainly an aspect of Identity—when I first encountered the statues and legends of William Wallace.

I have been conflicted about how I view the issue of Self. The phrase "a sense of self" seems mostly positive; "selfish" is certainly not. When I take an inventory of my own traits, when I'm considering my Self, I observe some aspects we wouldn't normally think of as benevolent. I'm profoundly stubborn. I'm quick to judge and can be slow to forgive. I'm competitive and prideful more often than I want to admit.

But are these—*any* of these attributes—really bad? The answer is, it depends. I love the biblical wisdom: "All things work together for good to those who love God."[2] When I first began working with Mel Gibson, when the preproduction period for the movie began, I had a wonderful sense of respect and even awe for his talent and accomplishments. He was younger in years than I was, but older in the movie business. He had proven his talents and passions many times already, and I was an unknown quantity, even to myself.

What struck me immediately about him was the intensity of his focus and depth of his commitment. I wasn't remotely in his universe, in terms of stature or measureable accomplishment, yet he asked me questions and listened to my responses with openness and sincerity. He wasn't quick to trust people, and that made me all the more appreciative that he trusted me.

I knew I was in the Big Leagues. And I have confidence, generally. But one of my first coaches taught me that to overestimate the obstacles you face and underestimate yourself will generally work in your favor. As *Braveheart* began, I had some Dark Nights of the Soul.

I found myself on my knees in prayer. During that time, I had a Revelation; I prayed: "Lord, I know I'm proud and prideful. This is how I am right now in life, and this is how I am to this point where you have brought me. I pray to trust that you can and will use everything I am and everything I have—including all the things I might not like about myself—as tools to do whatever it is that you want."

This was the deepest approach I took to the making of *Braveheart*. I don't know what Mel (or anyone else) prayed about it; I only know for sure that Mel, too, said his own prayers, and the movie became what it has become.

And what has it become? I have only my own perspective. I know that in Scotland there is a whole political movement that calls itself the Bravehearts. I know that people in different cultures all over the world have responded to the story. I know that words I wrote have been repeated all over the world. "Every man dies; not every man really lives" has been said more times than I could guess, especially at funerals. Maybe the most-repeated line of all has been "Freeeeeedommmm!"

But there is an aspect in what has happened that strikes me in the issues of Self and Pride. People quote the lines of the movie and attribute them to William Wallace. I identify so strongly with the man I take to be my ancestor and with the movie the Spirit spawned in me. I have absolutely no proof—not of the sort that would be considered scientific or legal—to claim a direct biological lineage. All of my sense of relationship to William Wallace is based on a spiritual experience.

In both the legal and the scientific sense, I am the author of those words that people quote. Authors have written books and repeatedly quoted words I wrote, attributing them to William Wallace. On the wall of the Air Force Academy are these words:

> And dying in our beds many years from now, would you not trade all the days from that day to this for one chance, just one chance, to come back here and tell our enemies that they may take our lives, but they'll never take our FREEDOM!

And just below those words is inscribed *William Wallace.*

My William Wallace said that. No other William Wallace, including the historical one, is recorded as having said anything resembling that.

To my ego, this doesn't seem fair. Writers know that words are written, and they should know—at least so my Self says—that they should be honestly attributed.

But the process of wrestling with all this has prodded me toward a Transformation that may involve the death of Self and the life of Spirit.

I believe that process has been going on throughout all my life, and through everyone else's too. For me, one of the biggest battles of my life occurred when *Braveheart* was nominated for a whole basketful of Academy Awards.

I don't like talking about this; to this day, it makes me feel petty. I'll try to describe this honestly—pettiness and all.

To be nominated for an Oscar is to be swept up into a swirl of attention that no other experience could have prepared a person for, especially if that person is a writer and has worked in solitude for years.

It isn't just that a massive publicity machine is spinning at a frantic rate and considers you a part of its fuel or its fodder; the bigger machine is the personal one. Family, friends, acquaintances, and total strangers get swept up in it too, and feel connected to the process. They *are* part of the process in that we humans are hardwired as herd animals.

A friend of mine who is a scientist as well as an artist explained it to me. He said that a herd has a collective consciousness that isn't fully understood but can be easily observed. If a herd is grazing peacefully and predators appear nearby—take, for example, a herd of wildebeests being stalked by lions—the wildebeests nearest the lions will notice them first, but fear ripples through the herd at such an instantaneous rate that those farthest from the lions will begin to run first. *All* of them experience the fear of the lions, and this helps them survive.

When awards season begins in Hollywood, the awards begin to be thought of as a matter of life and death, and that sense begins to ripple through everyone. The nominations are announced and discussed across the world. And when the time comes for the Oscar broadcast, more than a billion people are likely to be watching.

This has an effect on people. It's a tidal wave of attention that builds as it sweeps more and more individuals into its collective hold. This isn't to say that it is its own entity, evil unto itself. Awards of any kind are traditions that have grown out of our natural pride and ego and our drive to look out for who is popular.

This isn't new. The impulse that drives it is so powerful and so potentially destructive that it is its own sin: Idolatry.

If my friend Jill Conner Browne is right—and she always is—all the biblical commandants boil down to one: "I am the LORD your God . . . [and] you shall have no other gods before Me."[3]

The Academy Awards, and all the others that crave to be just like them, can be the literal worship of the Golden Calf. All the tools that go into the practice of storytelling—drama, humor, music, dance, dazzling images—are used to create the wave that is meant to sweep people up and convince them that what happens at the Oscars is something of massive significance.

Laird Hamilton is someone else I am proud to call a friend. He has accomplished so many original feats of skill and daring that those of us who know him refer to astounding courage as "going all Laird." He was the pioneer in the riding of waves so large that to approach them on a surfboard was thought to be suicide. Laird says, "Awards are never given for the sake of the person receiving them; they're completely for the sake of the person giving them."

Laird's observation is as true about the Oscars as it is about everything else. The irony is that the people on the receiving end are, it seems to me, artists who do everything they can to keep their craft sacred. Sometimes this extends to avoiding awards altogether. A few of the most recognized actors in the world have chosen not to be present when they were presented with Academy Awards, and I can only think that they were trying to keep their art pure by avoiding the waves of Idolatry.

When *Braveheart* was nominated, I was nominated, too, for Best Original Screenplay. While I tried not to anticipate, I couldn't avoid the sense that I would be given the Oscar. I was the only one in the category of Original Screenplay who had written a movie that was also nominated in the category of Best Picture.

The award went to someone else.

It may have been the best thing that could have happened to me, and for me.

It sure didn't feel like that at the time.

I never watch the Academy Awards. I had no interest in them before my *Braveheart* experience, and I have less interest now since I've experienced how toxic they can be. But I freely admit I had begun to want the Oscar and was deeply disappointed when that didn't happen.

What this forced in me was growth.

I knew, with the kind of absolute certainty I felt when in my life's most sacred Moments, that if I lived for the praise of the crowd and the approval of others, I was lost. I don't think anyone else can take another person's soul; our soul can only be surrendered. It is not part of us—it *is* us.

This was easy to know and hard to remember. It is hard enough to follow your own calling; it is harder still when you are facing a river of people running in the opposite direction screaming, "This way! Follow us!"

I believe the one who served most as Teacher, Warrior, and Sage in this lesson was my Mother. When I had left home to become a writer, she had given me a cup showing a young man, seated and staring away into the distance, with this inscription: "If a man does not keep pace with his companions, perhaps he marches to the beat of a different drummer."

My Father's basic message in life was to do everything possible to please a customer—but "possible" did not include doing the wrong thing. He sometimes told me, "If our customers don't prosper, we starve." And for him, to prosper meant to live an ethical life. Daddy liked everyone and expected everyone to like him. Mama's perspective was somewhat different. She believed—and taught me—that if everyone liked you, you were doing something wrong.

I believe it was Descartes who said, "In a world of fugitives, the man who does not run away will be perceived to flee." I'm sure that I seemed to some friends and family, and even to myself, to be running from the Business. But I already had the foundation, and I knew in my bones that the Braveheart Spirit had begun showing itself in my life when I had been on my knees to God.

Was my ego dead? Of course not. Was my Self dead? I was more alive than ever, even in isolation and pain.

And I was not alone at all. There were friends there, and family. I just had trouble letting them in. One of the best moments of the whole experience came from two phone messages from Andrew, my eldest son. He was on an elementary-school trip to Washington, DC, when the biggest of the awards nights happened. His school was full of children whose parents were entertainment business professionals, and Los Angeles is a company town, where everyone's direct or indirect connection to movies amplifies their fascination for the golden statues.

On the night of the Oscar broadcast, the teachers and chaperones of the class trip had gathered the children around a television to watch Andrew's father win. I can imagine that room, with dozens of ten-year-olds expecting to hear Andrew's dad's name announced. It wasn't. What did that feel like to my son?

I don't know. What I do know is that he called twice, the day after the broadcast, to ask if I was all right. And I would always know that my son had a Braveheart.

Not everyone did, at least not that I could see. I had the horrible feeling that many people around me were deeply disappointed—not for me, but for themselves. *They* felt cheated that I didn't win. To this day I've never known how to sort this out.

I told myself that all that mattered was what was in front of me, not what was behind. If I never wrote anything else, then I had truly fallen on my knees to the Golden Idol, and had let that dead process be the judge of my life.

We say, "Be yourself." But what Self do we mean? The one that cowers in fear or the one that acts in faith? A Spirit had led me to *Braveheart*; would I stop believing and listening to that Spirit?

AND SUDDENLY, IT ALL MADE SENSE.

I could find a way to doubt almost everyone and everything in my life. I couldn't find a way to doubt Jesus.

Friends I love and respect deeply have asked me, "Why do you believe what you believe?" I think what they're really asking is, "*How* do you believe?"

What I've discovered is that I can't find a way *not* to believe, once I saw it this way: I can doubt everyone else. Jesus is different. There is something in him that isn't in the rest of us. I think what I'm seeing is what the writer of the Gospel of John saw. He's the one who began his story of Jesus by saying, "In the beginning was the Word, and the Word was with God, and the Word was God."⁴ Try for just a moment to see it the way John saw it—and I acknowledge this is a mystical argument. Jesus is in Heaven. He is so much a part of God that the only way to explain it is to say he *is* God. He comes here and suffers utterly—suffers not just in physical pain but in the greater pain of separation from God.

And does it completely for you and for me.

What greater love could there be than that?

SO NOW I WILL TELL YOU OF MY FATHER'S GIFT, THE LAST moment I was with him on earth.

I had not flown back to Virginia for his surgery. Everyone, including Thurman, had told me it would be routine and there was no need for me to interrupt my work on the final stages of finishing the movie. But when the pneumonia began, and he went into the coma, I came.

For several weeks I flew back and forth between Los Angeles and his hospital room in the intensive care unit of the Lynchburg General Hospital in Virginia. On my first visit back, he did not open his eyes at all. But we still had hope that he would. He was a fighter, and he was still fighting.

The second weekend I flew back, it had begun to dawn on all of us who loved him that he might not wake and that we had seen his eyes and his smile for the last time.

I was in his hospital room at his bedside, about to head back to the airport, when he stirred. He lifted his head, opened his eyes, and turned toward me.

He could not speak. The breathing tube down his airway had made his throat too raw for words to come out, even if he had words to say. But he didn't need them.

His eyes on mine, he touched his heart.

ALL OF US DIE.

And all of us can really live.

Amen.

NOTES

INTRODUCTION: THE FREEDOM TO SCREAM
"FREEEEEEDOMMMM!"
1. John 8:32 KJV.

FIVE: A CALLING—AND A PIANO-PLAYING PIG
1. Joseph Campbell (1904–87), American mythologist, author, and lecturer, is probably best remembered for his "follow your bliss" philosophy.

SIX: BOB FROM AFGHANISTAN
1. Matthew 18:20, author's paraphrase.

TWELVE: CONNECTING
1. Kahlil Gibran, *Sand and Foam*, ed. Will Jonson (Seattle: CreateSpace, 2014), 10.

SEVENTEEN: THE BRAVEHEART LIFE EMBRACES MYSTERY
1. Psalm 8:4 KJV.
2. Luke 12:7, 24.

EIGHTEEN: A WARRIOR BELIEVES
1. Confrontation between Robert the Bruce and his father.
2. William Wallace replies to Princess Isabelle when she visits him in prison before his torturous execution.
3. Mark 14:29, author's paraphrase.

4. Mark 14:30.

5. Luke 22:31–32.

6. See Luke 11:2; Galatians 4:6; Romans 8:15.

7. Matthew 6:28–29.

Nineteen: My Daddy's Gift

1. "The Mansions of the Lord," words by Randall Wallace (music by Nick Glennie-Smith), © 2002 Songs of Wheelhouse.

Twenty: In Defense of Fear

1. 1 John 4:16.

2. C. S. Lewis, *Mere Christianity* (San Francisco: HarperSanFrancisco, 2015), 103.

3. Romans 8:28.

4. John 10:10, author's paraphrase.

Twenty-One: The Fears of Women

1. Romans 8:28.

2. Poem by Ben Jonson, a contemporary of William Shakespeare. Jonson was an English poet, dramatist, and actor. Ben Jonson, XLVII "Still to be neat," *Ben Jonson: The Complete Poems*, ed. George Parfitt (New York: Penguin Classics, 1996), 258.

Twenty-Two: Fear's Greatest Lie

1. Exodus 3:14, author's paraphrase.

2. As examples, see Daniel 10:12; Matthew 1:20; and Luke 1:30.

3. Hebrews 13:2 kjv.

Twenty-Three: Losing Our Identity

1. "It's Who You Are," words and music by Randall Wallace, © 2009 Songs of Wheelhouse.

2. Acts 3:6 kjv.

3. Matthew 6:28–29 kjv.

4. "When the Midnight Turns to Rose," words and music by Randall Wallace, © 2015 Songs of Wheelhouse.

5. "I Am Resolved," words by Palmer Hartsough (music by James Fillmore), 1896.

6. "The Hymn of Joy" (also called "Joyful, Joyful We Adore Thee"), words by Henry van Dyke (written to Ludwig van Beethoven's "Ode to Joy," the final movement of Symphony No. 9), 1907.
7. Luke 22:42 KJV.

Twenty-Seven: the Braveheart Life
1. Psalm 23:4 KJV.
2. Romans 8:31 KJV.
3. John 12:32 KJV.
4. John 14:6 KJV.

Twenty-Eight: Where Do You Put Your Guns?
1. Lt. General Harold G. Moore and Joseph L. Galloway, *We Were Soldiers Once . . . and Young* (New York City: Random House, 1992), xxiv.

Twenty-Nine: So Who Goes to Heaven?
1. C. S. Lewis, *The Screwtape Proposes a Toast* in *The Complete C. S. Lewis Signature Classics* (Grand Rapids, MI: Zondervan, 2007), 291.
2. Randall Wallace, "A Poor Girl's Child," © 1999 Randall Wallace. All rights reserved.

Thirty-One: Ego
1. Matthew 16:24 KJV.
2. Romans 8:28.
3. Exodus 20: 2–3.
4. John 1:1.

About the Author

RANDALL WALLACE IS A SCREENWRITER, DIRECTOR, PRODUCER, novelist, and songwriter who rose to prominence through his original screenplay for the film *Braveheart*. His work on the movie earned him an Oscar nomination for Best Original Screenplay and a Writers Guild of America award for Best Screenplay Written Directly for the Screen.

In addition to *Braveheart* Wallace is also the writer and/or director behind *The Man in the Iron Mask*, *We Were Soldiers*, *Pearl Harbor*, *Secretariat*, and *Heaven Is for Real* movies, which celebrate the value of faith, courage, and honor.

Wallace graduated from Duke University and put himself through a year of divinity school by teaching karate. In addition to his work as a filmmaker, he has authored nine books, is the founder of Hollywood for Habitat for Humanity, and is the father of three sons.